CONTENTS

*I*NTRODUCTION

This book is written primarily for pupils studying Standard Grade Modern Studies. The book is structured in such a way as to allow teachers to follow a complete chapter or to select individual units as appropriate.

The authors have attempted to provide a wide range of different material and exercises, but the book requires a considerable amount of teacher input and should not be seen as a stand-alone source or a complete course. While a variety of questions (based directly on the resources provided) and activities (designed as extensions to the book) is provided, teachers will wish to adapt and develop some of the ideas in the book to suit their own classroom needs. It is hoped, however, that teachers will find the examples provide a useful starting point both in terms of content and skill-based activities.

Britain is designed to provide a balance between a traditional text-book with links and continuity through the text, and a range of source material, written and visual, to suit the requirements of pupil-centred activities in Standard Grade. A range of exercises suitable for pupils of all abilities is provided, although a conscious decision has been made that these should not be designated 'credit', 'general', or 'foundation'. While many of the resources and exercises are suitable for 'foundation' level pupils, the majority are aimed at pupils studying for the 'general' and 'credit' levels.

Within each Unit, a list of the essential Keywords encountered in the Unit is given to ensure that all pupils are aware of the key ideas covered in the Unit. The range of activities throughout the book is designed to provide examples of good practice, e.g. in letter writing, questionnaire design, interviewing and role play. Through these activities, pupils will gain experience of the essential elements of evaluating, investigating and participating which are central to Standard Grade Modern Studies.

The 'Arrangements in Standard Grade Modern Studies' published by the Scottish Examination Board recognise that, 'the ultimate goal of the subject is for pupils to use, in a constructive way, acquired knowledge and skills and, therefore, emphasises attitudes and values which help prepare pupils for participation in the social and political situations which they will meet in their adult lives.' The authors of *Britain* have attempted to provide a resource which, together with the necessary teacher input, will assist pupils to achieve this goal.

O & B MODERN STUDIES

BRITAIN
PEOPLE, POLITICS AND SOCIETY

Jim Cannon

Principal Teacher of Modern Studies,
Craigmount High School, Edinburgh

Bill Clark

Formerly Head Teacher
Galashiels Academy

Gus Mackenzie

Principal Teacher of Modern Studies,
Deans Community High School, Livingston

George Smuga

Depute Head Teacher
Beeslack High School, Penicuik

Oliver & Boyd

Acknowledgements

The authors and publishers wish to thank all those who gave their permission for the reproduction of copyright material in this book. Information regarding the sources of extracts is given in the text. Photographs and other pictorial material are acknowledged as follows:

Courtesy Aid-Call PLC. Emergency Medical Alarms, p.95; Anti Apartheid (Scottish Committee), p.67; British United Provident Association (BUPA), p.99; Canon (UK) Ltd, p.118 (bottom); J Allan Cash Photolibrary, p.53 (both), 120 (top), 121 (both), 122 (top two); Central TV, p.118; Courtesy The Children's Society, p.79; Conservative Central Office, p.56; Dundee Courier and Advertiser, p.121; Eurotunnel/QA Photos Ltd., © Trans Manche Link, p.124; *Evening News*, Edinburgh, p.82; *Evening Times*, Glasgow, p.65; *Fishing News*, pp.122 (bottom), 123; Ford Motors, p.118 (top left); John Frost International Newspaper Service, p.23; Gateway Foodmarkets Ltd, p.120; Greenpeace, p.74; Help the Aged, p.104; Industrial Disease Sufferers' Group, p.67; The Labour Party, p.57; Miele Company Ltd, p.118 (middle right); Henry McLeish MP, p.37; NCR Ltd, pp.118 (top right), 120 (middle); National Council for Civil Liberties (NCCL), p.67; National Viewers and Listeners Association (NAVLA), pp.70–1; © *The Observer*, pp.73, 75, 87; The Photo Co-op, pp. 10 (top right), 14 (bottom), 90; The Press Association, p.75; Rex Features, pp.14 (top), 72, 113 (both); Ricoh, p.118 (middle left); The Salvation Army, p.104; The Samaritans, p.104; Scotsman Publications, pp.32, 33, 39, 73, 85, 116 (both); Scottish Green Party, p.56; Scottish National Party, p.56; Shelter, p.104; Social and Liberal Democrats, p.58; The Spastics Society, p.67; Thomson Travel/British Rail, p.87; *Today*/Dave Gaskill, p.110, *Today*, p.121; Topham Picture Source, pp.10 (top right, bottom left), 57 (both), 58, 70, 121 (bottom); Wang (UK) Ltd, p.118 (top middle); Walter Chappell Music Ltd. and International Music Publications, p.115.

Oliver & Boyd
Longman House
Burnt Mill
Harlow
Essex CM20 2JE
An imprint of Longman Group UK Ltd

ISBN 0 05 004483 4
First published 1990

Typset on an Apple Macintosh SE30 in Times 11/13 pt.
Produced by Longman Group (FE) Ltd
Printed in Hong Kong

1

WHO DECIDES?
(DEMOCRACY AND ELECTIONS)

YOU'VE NO RIGHT...
(A short play in two scenes)

Characters

Third-year pupils: Alex, Karen, Lynne, Keith, Anwar and Ian
Fourth-year pupils: Craig, Rab and Stewart
Teacher: Mrs Wilson

Scene 1

The lunch bell has just rung at Craigford High School. A queue of pupils, mainly third-year, is forming beside the school cafeteria door, which is still closed. There is some friendly pushing and shoving for places.

Alex	"What are you having today?"
Keith	"I'm having the pizza and chips."
Anwar	"It's good being first in the queue. You get more choice."

(Suddenly, three fourth-year boys come up alongside the queue, and then push in at the front.)

Keith	"Hey! You can't push in there. We were here first."
Craig	"We've got a football meeting at 1 o'clock."
Karen	"That doesn't matter! We're first."
Craig	"It does matter. If we don't get in now we'll miss the meeting, and maybe won't be selected to play in the cup game tomorrow."
Alex	"It's not fair." (*Shouting*) "We were here first!"
Rab	(*Moving towards Alex, threateningly*) "So what! You got something to say about it?"
Third-year voices	"Leave him alone!"
Karen	"You've no **right** to push in. We were here first."

(Just then, the cafeteria door opens, and Craig, Rab and Stewart go in first for lunch.)

Scene 2

The third-year pupils involved in the lunch queue are going into their Tutor Group classroom, after lunch. Mrs Wilson, their Tutor, is at her desk. The pupils gather round the desk.

Karen "Mrs Wilson, do you think this is fair? Some fourth-years pushed in for lunch before us."

Anwar "They said they were going to a meeting and had to get in early."

Lynne "Can we go and see Mr Jones, the headteacher?"

Mrs Wilson "All right, but you can't all go. Two is enough, so you will have to decide for yourselves who is going to speak for you. They will be your **representatives**."

Keith "Which two are going to go?"

Lynne "You can go, you were at the front of the queue."

Anwar "No. You can't do that. Just because Keith was at the front, doesn't mean he can speak up for the rest of us. I think we should send Alex. He's the biggest, and he stood up for us against them."

All voices "Yes. Alex can go!"

Alex "Okay. But who else is going? Ian, you're the brainbox in the class. You should go."

Karen (*Indignantly*) "You can't just ask somebody because they're bigger or cleverer. What does Ian know about it anyway? He was at the back of the queue and couldn't have seen all that happened, so he couldn't say much about it."

Lynne "It doesn't matter whether he saw it or not, he could still put forward our views. I still think Ian should go."

Karen "Surely we can't send him. He hardly ever speaks. Anyway, we don't know how many others want him to go. We'll have to find out what other people in the class think about who should go."

Anwar "How can we find out that?"

Karen "We could find out who wants to go, then have a **vote** to decide which two should go."

Ian "How do we know who wants to go?"

Alex "Who wants to go?"

(*Six pupils volunteer:*)

Anwar "But Mrs Wilson said only two could go."

Karen "We'll have to vote to **elect** two people to go to see the headteacher."

Mrs Wilson "All right, then, listen carefully. There are six **candidates** and each person in the class has one vote. As I read out the name of each candidate, raise your hand if you wish to vote for that candidate. Lynne can count the votes and write the totals on the blackboard."

(*The voting and counting take place. Karen and Alex are elected to represent the class at the meeting with the headteacher.*)

At Craigford High School, it was later decided to set up a Pupils' Representative Council so that two pupil representatives from each year could attend a meeting with the headteacher, to raise any suggestions and take part (**participate**) in discussions and making decisions.

Alternative ending to scene 1

Keith "Hey! You can't push in there. We were here first."

Stewart "So what! We've got as much right as you."

Anwar "No, you haven't! We were here first."

Stewart "Oh, shut up! You third-year kids are just getting in the way." (*Pushes Anwar*)

Alex (*Pulling Stewart's arm*) "Hey! Stop that!"

Rab (*Grabbing Alex by the jersey front and pushing him against the wall*) "We warned you lot!" (*Shouting*) "The next one who tries to stop us gets it–right!"

Craig, Rab and Stewart glare menacingly at the third-year pupils then start to push through the queue towards the cafeteria. Some of the third-year pupils are pushed back against the wall as the fourth-year group reach the door. The third-year pupils start shouting and protesting. One of the teachers appears.

Teacher "Here! You fourth-years! Stop pushing through the queue. You can't barge in like that, the third-years were here first."

Rab "We're in a hurry. We've got a meeting."

Teacher "I don't care what hurry you're in, you can't behave like that. Now get to the end of the queue."

Q UESTIONS

1. Why were the third-year pupils angry about the fourth-year pupils jumping the queue?

2. What did the fourth-year boys give as their reason for jumping the queue?

3. Why did Karen say the fourth-years had no **right** to push in?

4. Write down, in your own words, a description of how the two class representatives were chosen.

5. Describe two other ways that class representatives might be chosen.

6. List four qualities you would look for in a good class representative, and give reasons why you have chosen these qualities.

A CTIVITIES

1. Discuss this dispute in a group, and decide what you think about the way it was handled.

2. Read the alternative ending to Scene 1.

3. Discuss this within your group. Do you think this would have been a better way to end the dispute? Write down your reasons.

4. Discuss four other possible disputes that might arise during a school day at Craigford.

5. Choose **one** of these possible disputes, write down how it might arise, and how it might be solved.

6. Discuss possible characters who might be involved in your chosen dispute.

7. Write a short drama scene based on the dispute you have chosen. (**Note** you must include the words: right, decision, agreement, vote, and representative.)

8. Read **or** act your scene to the other groups in the class.

KEYWORDS

The following Keywords are used in this Unit. Make sure you have understood what they mean.

right	vote	candidate
representatives	elect	participate

Local government in Scotland

Background information

For purposes of local government, Scotland is divided into nine Regions. Each Region is further divided into Districts. Lothian Region, for example, is sub-divided into the four Districts of Edinburgh, Midlothian, East Lothian and West Lothian. In addition there are three Island Authorities – Orkney, Shetland and the Western Isles – which combine the jobs of Region and Districts. Finally each District has numerous Community Councils which help to focus attention on more local affairs.

There are elections for all of Scotland's Regional, District and Community Councils. Regional and District elections take place in Scotland every two years on a Regional/District cycle. Councils are elected for four years. There were Regional elections in 1986 and District elections in 1988.

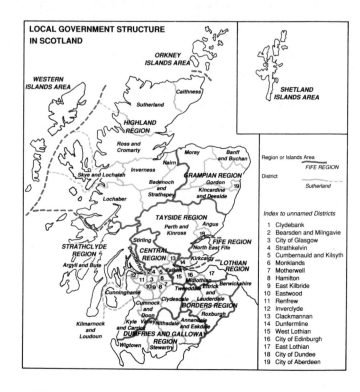

A Local Election - A Case Study

A Regional by-election is soon to be held in your area due to the death of a local councillor.

Before the by-election was announced, the Regional Council was divided as follows:

A CTIVITIES

1. Find out the name of the Region and the District in which you live.

2. Find out the names of your Regional and District Councillors and the political parties which they represent.

Labour, 12 councillors
Conservative, 13 councillors
Social and Liberal Democrats, 3 councillors
Scottish National Party, 3 councillors

The Regional Council was controlled by a combination of Conservative and SLD councillors.

Jack MacDonald - Conservative candidate - aged 43 - local businessman - garage owner.
Believes the main issue in the election to be that of controlling local council spending and argues that the reduction in council spending has been one of the achievements of the present Conservative-led Regional Council. Mr MacDonald hopes to retain this seat for the Conservatives.

David Wilson - Labour candidate - aged 35 - local government officer - active in trade union affairs.

Believes the issue of local services to be crucial. Due to cut-backs in spending, bus services and the state of repair to the local secondary school have been important local issues. He is hopeful that Labour's recent Parliamentary by-election win and good performance in the public opinion polls will help him to take the seat from the Conservatives.

Margaret Thomas - SLD candidate - aged 26 - community education worker - very much involved in local activities - member of the Community Council.

Believes that local issues should not be the subject of national political party game-playing. Thinks that the Regional Council has worked more moderately since neither of the two major parties has had an overall majority and has depended on the SLD for support.

Mary MacGregor - SNP candidate - aged 54 - lawyer - has stood for Parliamentary election.

Believes that Government handling of Scottish affairs is making the issue of Scottish independence an important one for local government.

Agrees with her party representatives on the Regional Council who have not supported the Conservative Group but would be prepared to support Labour if they became the largest group in the Council.

Local election campaign

We have met the four candidates for election in our Regional by-election. The candidates now face many hours of exhausting election campaigning as they try to persuade the public to **vote** for them. At the heart of the local campaign are the candidates and their party **agents**, who are either full-time professional party workers or experienced local members. The party agents use their political experience and local knowledge to help the candidates to make sure that supporters turn out to vote for their party.
What tactics can the candidate use?

Policies - Each candidate will of course have a set of policies or solutions to the major issues of the campaign. These will be set out in a 'policy statement' or election leaflet. It is on these issues that candidates will concentrate. Canvassing will help to establish which of the major issues most concern the voters.

A CTIVITIES

1. What are the local issues which are currently important in your own area? You will find these by looking at recent copies of your newspaper.

2. Either working individually or in groups, make use of your own local information and the background information given to design and write your own local newspaper article - 'Meet Your Candidates'. You should explain the importance for the Regional Council of this by-election, as well as bringing out the candidates' backgrounds and views on local issues. Try to write out first the sort of questions a journalist would ask the candidates about themselves and about local issues. If your teacher has access to a computer programme on newspaper lay-out make use of this to design and write your newspaper article.

Canvassing - This is the main campaign activity. Using information from the Electoral Register the candidate and party helpers visit a group of streets and ask local residents whether they will be voting for their candidate. When the candidate joins the canvassing team she/he will try to meet as many people as possible. The candidate's aim is to put himself or herself forward as the best person to represent the voters in the Council.

Getting out the vote - After canvassing and obtaining the maximum pre-election publicity for the candidate, the party helpers try to make sure that as many voters as possible cast their votes on the day. Cars will be arranged to take old or disabled people to the polling stations, and party workers may visit homes they have canvassed to see if promised supporters have actually voted. If they have not, the helpers may try to encourage them to do so.

Publicity - Each candidate tries to get as much publicity as possible. This is done through public appearances at local work places, shopping centres, old people's homes and also at special election meetings. Election leaflets are delivered by post and by party members, and posters are put up throughout the area. Party members are also encouraged to put up posters in their house windows. A few days before the election, and on election day, cars with loudspeakers will tour the area encouraging voters to vote for their candidate.

A CTIVITY: The Election Campaign Game

Rules: There are four candidates in this game. The class either splits into groups of four or into four large groups. Each individual or group will act the part of one of the candidates.

Each candidate starts with 30 points. Using a dice, proceed around the board collecting or losing points.

At the end of the game each group should list the factors which have affected their election campaign.

Discuss why the candidate who has finished with most points is in the best position to win the election.

THE ELECTION CAMPAIGN GAME

START

This is a safe seat for your Party. **COLLECT 10 POINTS**

You have a large number of volunteer Party helpers. **COLLECT 3 POINTS**

You have a very experienced Party agent. **COLLECT 5 POINTS**

Your Party has done well in a recent Parliamentary by-election. **COLLECT 3 POINTS**

Your local Party is badly organised. **LOSE 5 POINTS**

Canvassing shows that your policies are popular with voters. **COLLECT 4 POINTS**

Your Party has never won a seat in this area. **LOSE 10 POINTS**

Canvassing shows your Party has lost popularity. **LOSE 5 POINTS**

A local housing scandal gives bad publicity to your Party. **LOSE 4 POINTS**

A visit to an old people's home is given good coverage in the local press. **COLLECT 2 POINTS**

A national politician from your Party supports you at a public meeting. **COLLECT 2 POINTS**

You are a well-known local personality. **COLLECT 3 POINTS**

A public meeting you speak at is badly attended. **LOSE 2 POINTS**

Poor canvassing returns lead to low morale among Party workers. **LOSE 3 POINTS**

You make a number of well-publicised local appearances. **COLLECT 3 POINTS**

Late canvassing shows a move towards you from uncommitted voters. **COLLECT 4 POINTS**

Your Party workers make a major effort to get out your vote. **COLLECT 3 POINTS**

A national political problem badly affects your Party. **LOSE 5 POINTS**

Your main opponent appears in the local press, opening a new Health Centre. **LOSE 2 POINTS**

Your campaign starts to run out of money a week before the Election. **LOSE 3 POINTS**

An opinion poll shows a drop in support for your Party. **LOSE 5 POINTS**

An opinion poll shows your Party leading in the run-up to the Election. **COLLECT 5 POINTS**

It is raining on Election Day and you suffer from a low turn-out. **LOSE 4 POINTS**

Election Day

The procedure at elections is the same whether it is a local or a national election. Everyone over the age of eighteen who is a British subject has the right to vote. Each electoral area keeps a register of all people entitled to vote in that area. This is called the **Electoral Register**. When you are approaching eighteen it is important that you place your name on the Electoral Register, otherwise you will not be able to vote.

On the day of the election those who want to vote go to their local Polling Station to cast their vote. Before the day of the election all those on the Electoral Register will have received a voter's card which they should take with them when they go to vote.

Will your voice be heard on voting day?

The Electoral Register for 1989 is now being prepared. If your name's not on it you could be left without a say when it's time to vote.

Whom do you contact?

If you need to know more, or to obtain an application form, contact your Electoral Registration Officer. You'll find the address and telephone number at your nearest council office, post office, library or in the phone book.

Make sure of your vote.

Issued by the Scottish Office

THIS INFORMATION IS REQUIRED BY LAW   Representation of the People Acts

REGISTER of ELECTORS 1989

No one may vote at elections to Parliament, the European Parliament or local councils unless their name appears in a register of electors. A new register is produced each year and the law requires the householder to supply the information necessary to ensure that all eligible persons are included.

Please complete, sign and return the form as quickly as possible. **Do not wait until 10th October.**

You should complete the form even if you intend to move house after 10th October, 1988.

If no one in the household is eligible to be included in the register, please write 'NO ONE' and give an explanation in the appropriate Section.

REMEMBER: Only those in a Register of Electors are entitled to vote

Please complete Parts 1, 2, and 3 and sign the declaration (Part 4)

1 Address

No of flat, room or floor (where applicable)	No of house (or name if not numbered)	Name of street or road	Remainder of address including post code

2 Names

Enter in block capitals, the names of residents who are eligible to vote. Enter householder's name first, if resident and eligible.

		If 18 or over on 16th February, 1989 enter a ✓ in this column	16/17 YEAR OLDS If 18th birthday is after 16th February, 1989 and on or before the following 15th February, give date of birth		
SURNAME	FIRST FORENAME IN FULL, INITIALS OR OTHER FORENAMES.		DAY	MTH.	YR.
			/	/	
			/	/	
			/	/	

3 No one eligible

If no one in your household is eligible to vote, please write 'NO ONE' and give an explanation.

....

4 Declaration

I declare that to the best of my knowledge and belief the particulars given above are true and accurate, and that all those whose names are entered above are British citizens, other Commonwealth citizens or citizens of the Irish Republic, will be 18 or over by 15th February, 1990 and are eligible to be included in the register of electors.

Sign here: ....   Date ....

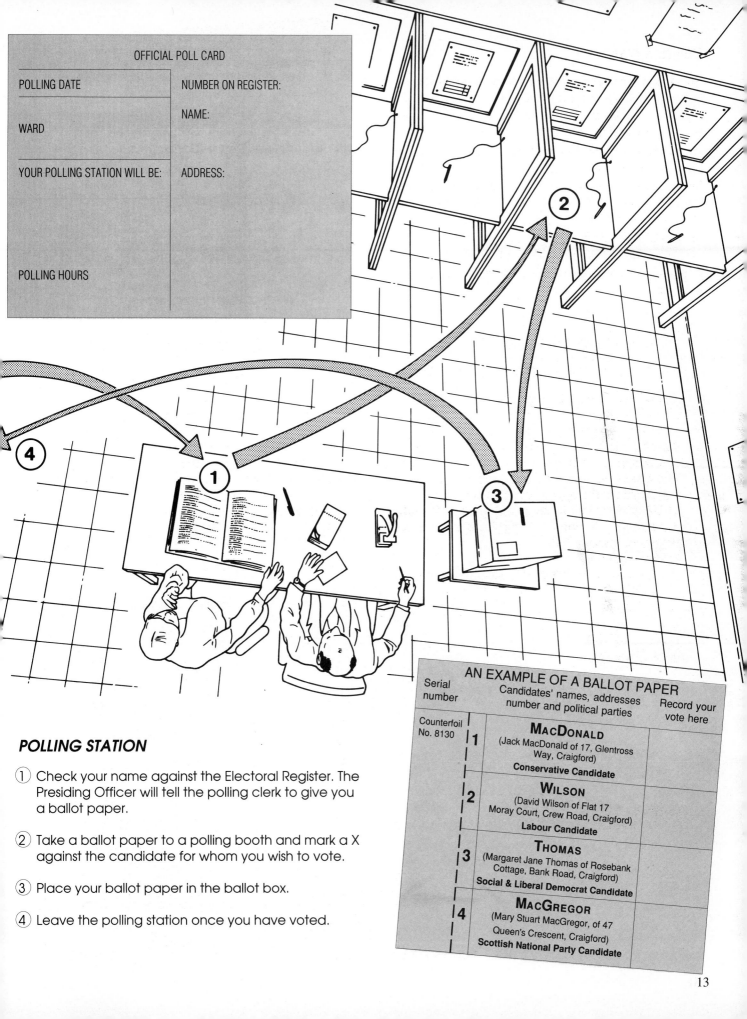

OFFICIAL POLL CARD

POLLING DATE

WARD

YOUR POLLING STATION WILL BE:

POLLING HOURS

NUMBER ON REGISTER:

NAME:

ADDRESS:

POLLING STATION

① Check your name against the Electoral Register. The Presiding Officer will tell the polling clerk to give you a ballot paper.

② Take a ballot paper to a polling booth and mark a X against the candidate for whom you wish to vote.

③ Place your ballot paper in the ballot box.

④ Leave the polling station once you have voted.

Serial number	AN EXAMPLE OF A BALLOT PAPER	
	Candidates' names, addresses number and political parties	Record your vote here
Counterfoil No. 8130	1 **MacDonald** (Jack MacDonald of 17, Glentross Way, Craigford) **Conservative Candidate**	
	2 **Wilson** (David Wilson of Flat 17 Moray Court, Crew Road, Craigford) **Labour Candidate**	
	3 **Thomas** (Margaret Jane Thomas of Rosebank Cottage, Bank Road, Craigford) **Social & Liberal Democrat Candidate**	
	4 **MacGregor** (Mary Stuart MacGregor, of 47 Queen's Crescent, Craigford) **Scottish National Party Candidate**	

The Result

When all the votes have been counted the Returning Officer announces the result.

"Ladies and gentlemen the votes cast in the election for the Regional district of . . . . were as follows:

Jack MacDonald (Conservative) 2693
Mary MacGregor (Scottish National Party) 798
Margaret Thomas (Social and Liberal Democrat) 1050
David Wilson (Labour) 2840

David Wilson has therefore been elected to serve as Councillor for the Regional district of . . . ."

The system of election used in the United Kingdom gives victory to the candidate who gains the single largest number of votes, no matter how many votes go to all the other candidates. This is known as a simple majority system and because it gives victory to the candidate with the most votes - no matter the size of the majority - it is often called the **'first-past-the-post'** system. To work out the majority by which a candidate wins, you take the largest number of votes cast and subtract the second largest number of votes - thus:

David Wilson	2840
Jack MacDonald	2693
Majority	147

Labour win in key by-election contest

Last night Labour Party officials celebrated an important victory in the Regional by-election caused by the death of a well known Conservative Councillor, Dick Forbes.

This victory now makes Labour the ruling group on the Council and the Labour Group are now expected to enter into discussions with the SNP who have said they will give Labour support on moves to improve local services. Winning candidate, David Wilson declared that "this was an important night for Labour and a clear indication from the voters that local services had suffered under the Conservatives".

Disappointed Conservative candidate, Jack MacDonald, accepted that "the issue of local services had been important" but saw this as a temporary set-back and believed "the Conservatives would regain the seat at the next Regional elections when voters would realise the costs of Labour control".

For the SNP and Social and Liberal Democrats the result was a disappointment with both candidates failing to improve their share of the vote.

(The Evening Courier)

Here are some actual results from the 1988 District elections.

– Aikenhead (*Glasgow District*)	L. Fyfe (Labour)	1605
	J.P. Johnson (SNP)	551
	A. MacKenzie (Conservative)	1294
– Murrayfield (*Edinburgh District*)	S. Deacon (Labour)	453
	I. Chisholm (SNP)	205
	C. Richard (Conservative)	2281
	E. Sams (SLD)	325
– Craigshill (*West Lothian*)	V. Cunningham (Labour)	613
	F. Anderson (SNP)	920
	I. Davies (Conservative)	156
– Links (*Edinburgh District*)	A. Morrison (Labour)	1055
	S. Wilson (SNP)	219
	K. Alexander (Conservative)	391
	E. Wardlaw (SLD)	1895

QUESTIONS

1. For each of the four 1988 District elections results state the winning candidate and calculate the majority by which the candidate won.

2. Explain why the victory for Labour candidate David Wilson in our by-election case study was so important for the work of the Regional Council.

3. Write a short victory speech which David Wilson might have made on the night of the election result. You will need to remember to thank supporters and party helpers. In your speech you will refer to the local issues you identified earlier in this exercise, and outline why you have won.

KEYWORDS

The following Keywords are used in this Unit. Make sure you have understood what they mean.

Region	policies
District	canvassing
Council	Electoral Register
Councillor	polling station
by-election	ballot paper
agent	'first past the post'

How to run an election in your class

In this section you will find some ideas about how to run an election in your own class. You may already have picked up ideas from the previous pages on local elections.

It is important that you decide in advance what kind of an election you are going to hold in your class. You can then choose from the ideas on the next two pages the ones that suit your needs.

Your teacher will have a good idea about what is possible in your particular situation. Listen carefully to what is said about the different ways of running an election in your class.

1. **A class election** - you can run an election for a class representative or for members of a Pupils' Representative Council (see page 28).
2. **Alongside a real election** - your class can run an election in your school at the same time as Local Government Elections (See Unit 2) or a General Election (See Unit 3) or a European Election. The next two pages will give you some ideas for this one. This can be done on quite a small scale, although it is possible to make it a big event involving the real candidates, public meetings and lots of voters.
3. **A mock election** - you can run this in your own class using existing party policies and local issues.

A CTIVITIES

1. Read about the different ways of running an election in your class.

2. Discuss in groups the good and bad points about each of them.

3. Report back to the other groups and to your teacher.

4. Decide which one you are going to try.

5. Draw up a checklist like the one below to show how your election is going to be run.

A simple Election

This is a simple way of running an election in your class. It can be carried out in about an hour and a half – if you have the time in one block – or you can run it during a week's lessons. The aim is to elect one person from the class to represent your ideas on a school council.

1. Discuss with your teacher four changes you would like to see in your school.

2. The class now has to elect one person to represent your views to the Pupils' Representative Council or to the headteacher.

3. Each candidate will have to make a short speech to the rest of the class to persuade people to vote for her or him. He or she will have a small group of helpers.

Checklist

Election organisation	**What you need**
	Volunteers
1) Candidates	
2) Nominations	Each candidate needs four people to nominate them
3) Candidate's helpers to produce	Groups of 4-6 pupils to help each candidate
a) Manifesto c) Posters	**Materials**: Paper, glue, scissors, pens
b) Short speech d) Rosettes	
4) Ballot papers	2 people to make up ballot papers
5) Ballot Box	1 person to make box
6) Voters Roll	2 people to compile a list of voters
7) Tellers	2 people to count votes
8) Returning Officer	1 person to supervise and announce result
9) Security	1 person to check that there is no cheating
10) Election	Everyone has 1 vote
11) Results	Announced by Returning Officer, followed by vote of thanks by successful candidate

Running a bigger election, Checklist
The Election
The Election is called

Are you going to tie in with a real election? If so, contact the actual candidates for your area:

— interview them
— use them as candidates for your election
— ask local party workers to be the candidate
— use members of the class as candidates

Nominations

— Prepare nomination papers for the candidates to sign with several proposers.

The election campaign

— Collect newspaper cuttings about the election
— Make up a newspaper based on your own election
— Make an audio or video tape about the election
— Carry out opinion polls about how people will vote

Polling day

Decide who is going to be able to vote, your class, your year group, the whole school?
— Make up an Electoral Register
— Absent voters - can they vote?
— Make up ballot papers
— Make up ballot boxes
— What will you use as a voting booth?
— Contact your local Returning Officers for advice.

Results

— How are you going to work out the results?
— How are you going to announce the results?
— Compare your results with national or local results
— Why do you think that people voted the way they did?
— Were there differences between different age groups?

The Candidates
Candidates are selected and nominated

— Find out how candidates are selected by political parties
— Make up groups to work on behalf of each of your candidates

You could have an election agent, publicity and party workers.

Party manifestoes published

Each party group should:
— Obtain copies of the party manifestoes.
— Collect information on party policies.
— Make up leaflets outlining party policies.
— Find out which policies are most important or most unpopular.

Running a campaign

— Produce leaflets, posters, stickers, and badges
— Carry out surveys to find out if people will vote for your candidate
— Hold a meeting with the candidates in the real elections
(Remember you will need somewhere large enough to hold a big meeting.)

Getting the voters out

— How long will voting last?
— Where will voting take place?
(During class time, break time, lunch time?)

Winning or losing

— Report back to the school, to your local paper, Newsround, 'Extra Election'.
— Thank people who helped
— Tidy up!
— What have you learned?

NATIONAL ELECTIONS

Introduction

We have seen in the previous chapter the procedures involved in electing representatives to serve us on our local councils. We have similar procedures to elect representatives to serve us at national level in Parliament in the House of Commons. These representatives are called **Members of Parliament** (MPs) and each Member of Parliament represents one area of the country called a **Constituency**. Therefore the pattern of **representation** which affects us is as follows:

Local	: Community Council	– Community Councillor
	: District Council	– District Councillor
	: Regional Council	– Regional Councillor
National	: House of Commons	– Member of Parliament

(As members of the European Community we also have representatives to serve us in the European Parliament) -   thus

International : European Parliament – Euro - MP.

A CTIVITY

From your work in the previous chapter, you may already know the name and party of your local District and Regional Councillors. Find out, now, with the help of your teacher, the name and party of your local MP and your Euro-MP. You can now set this out in the following table which shows your levels of representation.

Who represents me?

Local
1) My District is called . . . .
   My District Councillor is . . . .
   and belongs to the . . . . Party.
2) My Region is called . . . .
   My Regional Councillor is . . . .
   and belongs to the . . . . Party.

National
My Constituency is called . . . .
My Member of Parliament is . . . .
   and belongs to the . . . . Party.

International
My Constituency is called . . . .
My Euro-MP is . . . .
   and belongs to the . . . . Party.

Britain has 650 constituencies, each returning one Member of Parliament to the House of Commons. These 650 MPs are re-elected at least every five years at a **General Election**. The life of a Parliament is not fixed and the **Prime Minister** (head of the Government) may decide to hold a General Election at any time within a five-year period. If an MP dies or retires there is a by-election in his or her constituency to elect a new representative.

The voting procedure and the system of finding the winning candidate is the same at national as at local elections, i.e. General Elections in the UK are held on the 'first-past-the-post' system. In an election all candidates have to provide a deposit of £500, which is returned to them if they obtain five per cent of the total number of votes. The election campaigns are also similar, but television and the newspapers take much more interest in a General Election than in local elections.

Here are the results from two constituencies in the 1987 General Election.

Clackmannan – Total number of electors, 49 583

	Votes	% Votes
M.J. O'Neill (Lab)	20 317	53.8
A. Macartney (SNP)	7916	21.0
J. Parker (Cons)	5620	14.9
A. Watters (SDP/Alliance)	3961	10.5
Lab. Majority	12 401	

Turnout 76%

Ayr – Total number of electors, 67 224

	Votes	% Votes
G. Younger (Cons)	20 942	39.4
K. MacDonald (Lab)	20 760	39.1
K. Moody (Lib./Alliance)	7859	14.8
C.Weir (SNP)	3548	6.7
Cons. Majority	182	

Turnout 79%

Note

1. In these two results we are told the total number of electors on the Electoral Register in each constituency. By adding up all the votes cast we can work out how many people voted and by comparing this with the number of people entitled to vote we can work out the percentage **turnout** of voters.

2. If we add up the total number of votes cast for all the candidates we can calculate the percentage share of the vote for each candidate by comparing their number of votes with the total number of votes. By using this information we can record the share of the vote in a pie chart.

3. In the Clackmannan constituency the winning candidate had a large majority over his rivals. This is called a **safe constituency**. In the Ayr constituency the winning candidate had a very small majority. This is called a **marginal constituency**.

4. In the two constituencies no candidate lost his or her deposit because all candidates gained more than five per cent of the total number of votes.

A CTIVITIES

1. Here is one further constituency result from the 1987 General Election.

East Lothian - Total number of Electors, 65 603

J.D. Home Robertson (Lab)	24 583
S.M. Langdon (Cons)	14 478
A. Robinson (Lib./Alliance)	7929
A. Bugon-Lyon (SNP)	3727
A. Marland (Green Party)	451

a) Record the winning candidate and majority.
b) Calculate i) the percentage turnout
ii) the percentage share of the vote for each candidate
c) Record the percentage share of the vote as a pie chart.
d) State whether this is a **safe** or a **marginal** constituency.
e) Name any candidate who would have lost his or her deposit.

2. Find out from your teacher the result of the last election in your own constituency.
a) Who is your MP and what was his or her majority?
b) What was the percentage share of the vote for each candidate?
c) Record this as a pie chart.
d) Is your constituency a safe or a marginal one?
e) Did any candidate lose his or her deposit?

Forming a Government

As well as electing our MPs to represent us in Parliament, a General Election also decides the formation of the next Government. The Party with the largest number of MPs in the House of Commons becomes the Government and the leader of that Party becomes the Prime Minister. The Party with the second largest number of MPs becomes the **Opposition**.

When a Party has more MPs than all the other parties combined it is a **Majority Government**. When the largest Party does not have more MPs than all the other parties combined it is a **Minority Government**. Here are results for recent General Elections.

Year	Conservative	Labour	Liberal Liberal/SDP Alliance	SNP	Others	Total
1987	375	229	22	3	21	650
1983	397	209	23	2	19	650
1979	339	268	11	2	15	635
1974 (October)	277	319	13	11	15	635
1974 (February)	297	301	14	7	16	635

*Q*UESTIONS

1. For each General Election state which Party formed the Government and calculate what their overall majority was.

2. In which year was there a Minority Government?

A fair result?

Our voting system is very simple and straightforward and would appear to be fair in that the candidate in each constituency with the most votes is elected and the Party with the most MPs forms the Government. It is an essential part of any democracy that an elected representative and an elected Government have the support of the majority of the electors. The electors must feel the system is a fair one which enables their views to be properly represented.

Does the British system of elections meet these aims of **democracy**? Many people would argue that it does but others argue that it is not a fair system and is in need of reform.

An unfair system

There are two ways in which we can present the case against our electoral system.

1. *Is the result fair at constituency level?*
We have seen that in the 'first-past-the-post' system the candidate with the single largest number of votes is elected. E.g. In an imaginary constituency there are three candidates:

Mr Smith receives	24 683 votes
Ms Jones receives	21 496 votes
Mr Brown receives	18 103 votes

Mr Smith has the most votes and is elected with a majority of 3187 votes over his nearest rival. However, although 24 683 people voted for Mr Smith, 39 599 electors voted for other candidates. In other words Mr Smith does not have an overall majority and is not the choice of the overall majority of the electors. We can see this more clearly by comparing the results from two constituencies in the General Election of October 1974.

(i) **Dunbartonshire East**		
SNP	– 15 551	31.2% of total vote
Conservative	– 15 529	31.1% of total vote
Labour	– 15 122	30.3% of total vote
Liberal	– 3636	7.3% of total vote
(ii) **Rhondda**		
Labour	– 38 654	77.1% of total vote
Plaid Cymru	– 4173	8.3% of total vote
Conservative	– 3739	7.5% of total vote
Liberal	– 2142	4.3% of total vote
Communist	– 1404	2.8% of total vote

(i) Dunbartonshire East

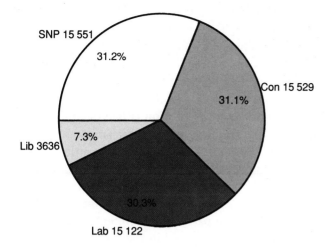

(ii) Rhondda

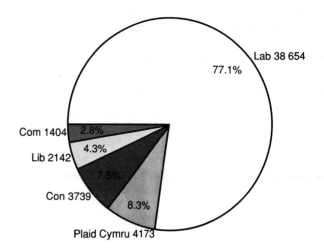

*A*CTIVITY

Write a short paragraph setting out the argument that the views of the electors were being represented in the Rhondda but not in Dunbartonshire East.

2. *Is the result fair at national level?*

We have seen that the Party with the largest number of MPs is allowed to form the Government. This again would seem to be a fair representation of the wishes of the electors.

But let us look again at some recent General Election results, this time showing the number of MPs and the percentage share of the vote.

Year	Conservative	% Vote	Labour	% Vote	Liberal: Liberal/SDP Alliance	% Vote	Others	% Vote
1987	375	42	229	31	22	23	24	4
1983	397	42	209	27.5	23	25.3	21	4
1979	339	44	268	37	11	14	17	4
1974 (October)	276	36	319	39	13	18	27	7
1974 (February)	296	38	301	37	14	19	24	6

*Q*UESTIONS

1. For the 1983 Election record separately for the Labour and the Alliance Parties the number of MPs elected, and compare these with the percentage of the vote gained by each Party.
2. For the 1974 (February) Election note which Party gained the largest number of MPs and note which Party gained the largest share of the vote.
3. For all Elections since 1974 note the percentage share of the total vote recorded by the winning Parties.

*A*CTIVITY

Use the answers to these three questions to write a paragraph arguing that our electoral system does not give a fair representation of the wishes of the electors.

Other ways of electing MPs

Other countries have different systems of electing representatives. One simple change to our system would be to replace 'first-past-the-post' with an **Alternative Vote** system. In this system we would keep our constituencies as they are but voters would be asked to show their preference, by putting a 1, 2 and so on against candidates. If a candidate received over 50 per cent of first preference votes then he or she would be elected. If not, then the bottom candidate would be withdrawn and his or her votes shared out amongst the other candidates until one candidate had 50 per cent of the vote.

We can see how this might work in our imaginary constituency where:

Mr Smith receives	24 683 votes
Ms Jones receives	21 496 votes
Mr Brown receives	18 103 votes

If this were an Alternative Vote system then the electors would have shown a second preference. No candidate has received over 50 per cent of the vote so Mr Brown is withdrawn and his second preference votes are shared out. Of the 18103 who voted for Mr Brown, 11 006 voted Ms Jones as second choice and 7097 voted for Mr Smith as second choice. When added to their original votes this means that Mr Smith now receives 31 780 votes and Ms Jones receives 32 502 votes, so Ms Jones is elected MP.

Alternative vote

Stanley John BODEN Labour Party	1
John V BUTTERFILL Conservative Party	5
John Michael FOSTER Scottish National Party	4
George MAJOR Green Party	2
William Henry PITT Social & Liberal Democrats	3

Party list

Conservative Party	
Green Party	
Scottish National Party	
Labour Party	
Social and Liberal Democrats	✗

The major advantage of this is that it makes sure each MP is the choice of more than half of the voters in his or her constituency and avoids such situations as the Dunbartonshire East result.

Another change would be to bring in a type of system where MPs are returned to Parliament in proportion to the share of the votes cast for their Party. Systems which produce results like these are described as **Proportional Representation (PR)** systems. There are various types of PR system but one simple form would be a National Party List system where parties produce lists of candidates and electors vote for parties and not candidates. If we have a Parliament of 400 MPs and a Party receives 25 per cent of the vote, then the first 100 candidates on that party's list become MPs. We can see what might have happened in 1983 if the UK had had a system of Party List in the following table:

Actual Result			Party List
Conservative	397 MPs	42.4% of vote	276 MPs
Labour	209 MPs	27.5% of vote	179 MPs
Liberal/SDP Alliance	23 MPs	25.3% of vote	165 MPs
Others	21 MPs	4.6% of vote	30 MPs
Total	650 MPs		

A CTIVITIES

1. Use the result from the table of the 1987 Election (page 21) and calculate what the result might have been under Party List.

2. Which Party (or parties) do you think might have formed the Government in 1983 and 1987 had we had a Party List System?
Discuss whether these Governments would have been strong Governments.

3. If you have carried out a classroom election, repeat the actual voting part, this time asking the voters to show on the ballot paper their first and second preference. Now calculate the result according to the Alternative Vote system and compare with your first result under 'first-past-the-post'.

4. Either as a whole class or in small groups discuss the issue of how fair the British electoral system is and whether we should replace it with an alternative.

The media and elections

During an election campaign a great deal of publicity is given to the political parties, their leaders and their policies by newspapers and by television. How do newspapers and television present the election? Are they fair to all parties? Do they influence the result?

Newspapers

Newspapers can be divided into various categories:

- local and national newspapers
- daily and Sunday newspapers
- 'popular' and 'quality' newspapers.

The most important newspapers during an election campaign are the national daily and Sunday newspapers. Most of these newspapers openly support one of the main political parties. In their support they can be very **biased** and do not need to be fair and balanced in their coverage of the election and of politics in general. The popular press in particular are very open in their party support and through their headlines, their articles and their use of photographs praise one political party and leader while attacking the other.

Newspaper support for the main political parties is not evenly divided among the political parties. For example, in 1987 Labour was supported by only 27 per cent of all the main daily national newspapers. The table on page 24 shows which political parties were supported by which main national daily and Sunday newspapers in the 1987 General Election.

PARTY SUPPORT AND THE NATIONAL PRESS *THE 1987 GENERAL ELECTION*

		CIRCULATION TO NEAREST '000	PARTY SUPPORTED
A	**POPULAR DAILY NEWSPAPERS**		
	Daily Express	1 677 000	Conservative
	Daily Mail	1 786 000	Conservative
	The Sun	4 195 000	Conservative
	Daily Star	1 006 000	Conservative
	Daily Mirror	3 132 000	Labour
	Today	502 000	Alliance
B	**QUALITY DAILY NEWSPAPERS**		
	Daily Telegraph	1 129 000	Conservative
	The Times	441 000	Conservative
	The Guardian	448 000	Labour
	The Independent	379 000	No one Party supported
C	**POPULAR SUNDAY NEWSPAPERS**		
	Sunday Express	2 088 000	Conservative
	The Mail on Sunday	1 913 000	Conservative
	News of the World	5 304 000	Conservative
	The People	2 764 000	Labour
	Sunday Mirror	2 862 000	Labour
D	**QUALITY SUNDAY NEWSPAPERS**		
	Sunday Telegraph	706 000	Conservative
	Sunday Times	1 348 000	Conservative
	The Observer	730 000	No one Party supported
E	**SELECTED SCOTTISH DAILY AND SUNDAY NEWSPAPERS**		
	Daily Record	774 000	Pro-Labour
	Glasgow Herald	123 000	No one Party supported
	Scotsman	89 000	No one Party supported
	Sunday Post	1 393 000	Pro-Conservative
	Sunday Mail	888 000	Pro-Labour

A CTIVITIES

1. Make use of the information in the table above to construct a bar chart to show the amount of support for the main political parties. Arrange the newspapers according to circulation figures. Once you have drawn your bar graph then colour code the various columns with blue for Conservative, red for Labour, yellow for the Alliance and white for those newspapers who were independent in their support. You may wish to construct several bar graphs showing daily and Sunday newspapers and 'popular' and 'quality' newspapers.

2. Total the overall number of daily national and Sunday national newspapers according to party support. Calculate these as percentages of the total numbers of newspapers given in the table and show your results in two pie-charts.

3. Here are two brief extracts from two popular newspapers just before the Election:

Extract A

'The Conservative Party exists to preserve its privileges. That is what it was created for. That is its historic role. The Labour Party was created to fight privilege, the degradation of poverty, the humiliation of unemployment, the misery of the slums. That is its historic duty.'

Say which political party each extract supports and give examples of the words and phrases which show this support.

4. Do this activity as a class exercise. Choose a selection of daily newspapers from the table to give examples of at least one Labour and one Conservative newspaper.

Study these newspapers for one day during the period when you are studying this topic. Put together a small project showing the main political story of that day, the headlines for that story, the photographs, etc. Highlight examples which show the newspapers' party support.

Extract B

'Are we really ready to accept Neil Kinnock's grotesque and contemptible caricature of today's Britain? He would have us believe that we are a down-trodden, hungry (yes, he has said hungry) crisis-ridden banana republic. His vision is warped by the class hatred that has suffused his and his party's campaign'

Television

Unlike the press, television is required by law to be politically fair and balanced and not to support any particular political party. Television companies can produce programmes concerned with politics and political issues but they cannot emphasise any political opinion of their own.

It is of course very difficult to remain neutral and balanced at all times and on occasions politicians and others will attack television for failing to be balanced. Norman Tebbitt, former Chairman of the Conservative Party, has criticised the BBC for presenting the news in a biased fashion whilst others have, for example, criticised television for being unfair to trades unions by always concentrating on strikes and on violent clashes during strikes. If a television news programme announces that 'workers have threatened to go on strike if management do not meet their pay demands' and that 'management have offered to discuss the pay claim' does the use of words like 'threatened', 'demand' and 'offered' present one side as being extreme whilst the other side is reasonable? These are difficult questions to answer and television producers are very aware of these difficulties.

How does television represent a General Election? There are various ways in which television presents coverage of a General Election.

- Daily news bulletins.
- Political and current affairs programmes such as *Panorama*, *World In Action*, *Newsnight*, etc.
- Political discussions such as *Question Time*.
- Party Political Broadcasts. Here television allows access to the political parties to broadcast their own short programmes. These are obviously in favour of one political party or another but to ensure some fairness all major political parties are allowed access. They do not, however, have the same broadcasting time. The amount of broadcasting time depends upon the votes polled by each party at the previous election. This obviously favours the Labour and Conservative Parties.
- Coverage of the actual Election night and the return and analysis of the results.

A CTIVITY

Study the television schedules for the week you are studying this topic and draw up a list of the main political and current affairs programmes shown on the various TV channels.

Public Opinion Polls

During an Election the results of public **opinion polls** are regularly presented on television and in the newspapers. Political parties anxiously await the results of these polls to work out whether public opinion is going their way or not. Some of the major polling organisations which publish opinion polls during an election are Gallup, MORI and NOP. Political parties also conduct their own opinion polls.

Politicians have very mixed public views about opinion polls. They refer to the opinion polls when their party is doing well but make critical comments about the polls when they show their party doing badly. Overall, however, politicians do take the result of public opinion polls seriously and are very careful in their analysis of opinion trends.

Do opinion polls affect election results? This is difficult to answer. If polls regularly show one political party ahead then this may encourage undecided voters to vote for it and may discourage other voters from voting for opposition parties. On the other hand it may make the leading party's supporters feel that the election is almost won and make them lazy about voting. In some countries public opinion polls are banned during the last few days of an election campaign.

Example of an opinion poll

POLL TAX

It is planned that domestic rates be abolished in Scotland and replaced with a flat rate charge of some £260* per person over the age of 18 in each household. On balance do you approve or disapprove of this change?

	Con	Lab	Dem/ SDP	SNP	All	All Sep '88
	%	%	%	%	%	%
Approve	58	7	25	11	19	24
Disapprove	36	90	75	88	77	70
No opinion	5	3	0	1	4	6

* Official Scottish Office average figure used in previous polls.
(source: MORI and *The Scotsman*)

At election time people who are organising election campaigns want to know about the popularity of the various political parties and how people intend to vote. Opinion polls or surveys have become an important part of campaigning. They can be taken on a whole range of issues, not always about politics, but during elections they are taken to find out how people are feeling about the main parties. They test the 'mood of the people'.

There are a number of important guidelines which have to be followed to ensure a successful opinion poll or survey.

First of all you must make sure of your objectives in doing the survey - you must be clear about what you are trying to find out.

Secondly you must make sure that the questions you ask are worded clearly, so that everyone can understand them, and that they are going to help you achieve the objectives of your survey. It is a good idea to avoid questions which encourage vague or open-ended answers. It is easier to calculate and analyse your results if your questions are worded so that they have a Yes/No/Don't know response or otherwise a very limited series of answers.

Next you must make sure that you question a cross-section of people in your interviews. This is known as a **sample** and should represent the age, sex and social mix of the group as a whole.

Finally you have to calculate your findings and present these in statistical or graphical form.

Here is a sample questionnaire which has been drawn up to find out the views of people on how Scotland is governed. Following it is an example of how the answers to two of the questions can be analysed and presented in graphical form.

Sample Questionnaire

Craigford High School Modern Studies Project

Name of pupil   *Date of Interview*

Details of Person Being Interviewed (if appropriate)

Male/Female

Age: Under 20 ☐
20 - 60 ☐
Over 60 ☐

Address

1. Are you satisfied with the existing arrangements and institutions for the government of Scotland?

   Satisfied ☐ **Not Satisfied** ☐ **Don't know** ☐

2. Which of these options for the government of Scotland do you most favour?

   (a) the existing arrangements and institutions ☐

   (b) a Scottish Assembly with the power to pass laws ☐

   (c) an independent Scotland ☐

3. If you ticked box (b) in question 2, do you favour a Scottish Assembly having the power to raise its own taxes?

   Yes ☐ **No** ☐

4. If Scotland became independent do you think Scotland would be better off or worse off economically?

   Better off ☐
   Worse off ☐

5. Which political party do you support?

   Thank you for your co-operation.

Sample Statistics

Pie chart showing possible responses to Question 1
Satisfied – 25%
Not satisfied – 65%
Don't know – 10%

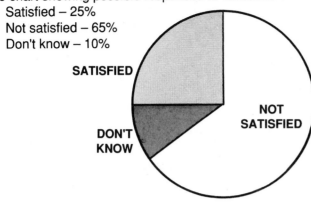

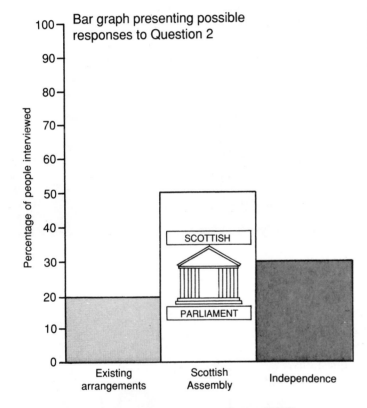

Bar graph presenting possible responses to Question 2

KEYWORDS

The following Keywords are used in this Unit. Make sure you have understood what they mean.

democracy
constituency
representation
General Election
turnout
safe constituency
marginal constituency
Government
proportional representation

Prime Minister
opposition
majority government
minority government
media
opinion poll
sample
bias

A CTIVITY

Working either in pairs or in small groups devise your own opinion poll or survey, carry out the research and present your findings in statistical or graphical form.

You will first have to decide on an issue – it need not be a political issue, it can be a local or a school issue.

Devise your questionnaire, including no more than five questions.

Carry out your interviews – this can be done in school or at a local shopping centre or community centre. Remember to ask a cross-section of people. You must always be polite in this and never press anyone if they do not want to answer your questions (for example about personal finance). Finally, for the purposes of this exercise, limit yourself to a small survey – 20 to 25 people. This will help you in calculating your findings.

It is a good idea to ask your teacher to give you a letter or card explaining that your survey has the approval of your school. The following simple letter is an example of what could be provided:

Dear Madam/Sir
James White, a pupil of Craigford High School, is conducting a survey as part of his work in Standard Grade Modern Studies. Your co-operation in completing this questionnaire would be much appreciated.

J. R. McLeod
Modern Studies Dept.
Craigford High School.

2

REPRESENTATION

UNIT UNIT UNIT UNIT UNIT UNIT
2.1
UNIT UNIT UNIT UNIT UNIT UNIT

WHAT'S YOUR VIEW?

As a result of the complaints about the lunch queues, and various other grumbles by pupils, the Headteacher decided to set up a **Pupils' Representative Council** at Craigford High School so that pupils could meet the Headteacher and discuss any problems.

(A short play)

Characters

Third-year Pupils: Alex, Karen, Lynne, Keith, Anwar and Ian.
Teacher: Mrs Wilson.

Scene 1

Mrs Wilson is explaining to her class what the Pupils' Representative Council is, how it will be set up and what it can do.

Mrs Wilson "The headteacher would like to set up a Pupils' Representative Council so that he can hear the views of pupils. Each year is to choose two pupils to go on to the Council to **represent** the views of the pupils of that year. So he will want two from Third-year. Now! Any questions?"

Anwar "How can two people represent all the Third-year? How will they be chosen, anyway?"

Mrs Wilson "There are only two from each year because the headteacher can't possibly meet *every* pupil in the school to discuss things with them all. He just does not have the time, so that is why only two pupils will represent each year. We have to choose two from those who say they want to be representatives."

Karen "But how can we choose from the whole year when we don't know lots of people in other classes. We might not even have seen some of them!"

Mrs Wilson "That's true! But how else can you select **representatives**? Anyway, that's what's been decided in this school – the whole of each year will vote for two representatives."

Ian "Well, at least everyone gets a chance to vote. What use would it have been if two from each year had just been selected by the headteacher to be on the Council!"

Alex "How are these representatives going to be able to put forward the views of the Third-year? I mean, how will they know what the Third-year think?"

Lynne "We could speak to them at break or write a letter to them so that they could find out things we wanted to be talked about at the Council meeting."

Karen "Yes. That's right. If we don't tell the representatives what we want, then they might just put forward their own views, then they would only be speaking for themselves."

Keith "Yes. What if they say nothing or maybe not what we wanted them to say. How will we know?"

Mrs Wilson "There should be some notes, called **Minutes**, taken at every Pupils' Representative Council meeting. These Minutes will contain some parts of what people said, and what decisions have been taken. You will then be able to read these Minutes or your representative can report back to you directly, telling you what was said and decided at the meeting."

*Q*UESTIONS

1. Why could all pupils not be on the Pupils' Representative Council?

2. What complaints could there be about having only two representatives for the whole year?

3. List as many ways as possible for the elected representatives to find out what other people's views are.

*A*CTIVITIES

1. Allocate parts and read the play.

2. *Group work*

a) Investigation. Find out the difference between a **Representative** and a **Delegate**.

b) Discussion/Illustration. How could you illustrate, using a flow chart diagram, two ways of electing representatives? For example the method at Craigford School was:

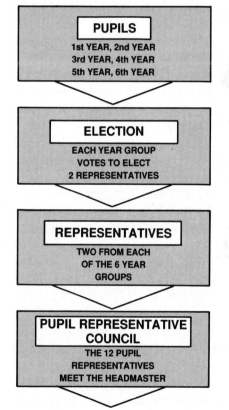

c) Discussion. List several ways in which a candidate in the year election at Craigford could make himself/herself known to the rest of the year group.

d) Illustration. Select one of your group as a candidate. Prepare a variety of publicity items to make your candidate better known to the rest of the class.

e) Investigation. Find out as much as you can about *Hansard*.

KEYWORDS

The following Keywords are used in this Unit. Make sure you have understood what they mean.

Pupils' Representative Council
represent
representatives
Minutes
delegate

WE DON'T NEED YOU ANY MORE!

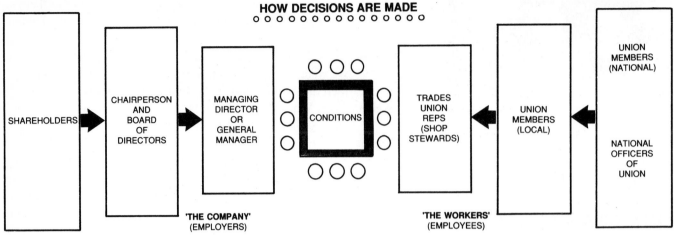

HOW DECISIONS ARE MADE

SHAREHOLDERS → CHAIRPERSON AND BOARD OF DIRECTORS → MANAGING DIRECTOR OR GENERAL MANAGER → CONDITIONS ← TRADES UNION REPS (SHOP STEWARDS) ← UNION MEMBERS (LOCAL) ← UNION MEMBERS (NATIONAL) / NATIONAL OFFICERS OF UNION

'THE COMPANY' (EMPLOYERS) **'THE WORKERS'** (EMPLOYEES)

Making decisions in industry

The diagram shows the traditional view of how decisions are made in factories, offices, shops and other parts of industry. The Managing Director or General Manager is the representative of the Board of Directors who, in turn, represent all the people who have bought shares in the company.

The trade union representatives in the company, sometimes known as **shop stewards**, put forward the views of the workers in the company who are members of the trade union. The two groups of representatives meet together to discuss any issues which affect them in the running of the company. Some of these issues might be the following:

Employers	Employees
Want to speed up production	Want improved safety conditions
Want to take on more people	Want to increase members' wages
Want to change a product	Want to change holiday arrangements
Want to close all or part of the factory	Want to protect members' jobs

The management representatives will want to reach a decision which is best for the company and its shareholders, while the trade union representatives will look after the interests of its members.

Every day in offices, shops and factories all over the country, decisions are agreed between the managers and workers without any disagreements or disputes. The development of good **industrial relations** between the two sides in industry is seen as very important by many companies and many trades unions. Many workers and trades union members know that if they are to continue to have jobs and be paid reasonable wages the company has to run as smoothly as possible. The managers know that if the company is to prosper, they have to treat their employees reasonably to avoid any interruption in production.

In these circumstances a fair approach is usually adopted by all those involved in the **negotiations**. The decision reached is a compromise agreed by both sides with benefits for both of them.

If there is a disagreement which cannot be solved the two sides may decide to call in a 'referee' to discuss the problem with them. This is known as **arbitration**. The Advisory, Conciliation and Arbitration Service (ACAS) is a Government body set up to help to solve major industrial disputes.

In some extreme cases where no satisfactory decision has been reached, the trades union members may take **industrial action**. The different kinds of action they take are shown in the box. Sometimes the management of a company are dissatisfied with workers' actions and this can lead to a 'lock-out'. The factory is closed and the workers are not allowed in to work even if they want to.

The disputes which make headline news in the newspapers and on television are the exceptions rather than the rule in the everyday running of industry. Nevertheless they are extremely important because they usually happen when there are major decisions to be made or major problems to be solved. When this happens the representation of members' views by their trades union representatives and the representation of the company's policies by the managers become even more important because the two sides are in conflict.

Trade union actions

Method	Actions
Work to rule	Work is carried out in accordance with every minor rule
Go slow	Workers will take their time
Closed shop	Workers will only work with fellow trade unionists
Demarcation dispute	It is insisted that only a trained worker will do a job that could be done by another
Strike	If wage negotiations break down completely, trade unions will withdraw their labour
Picketing	Strikers' representatives dissuade employees who do not wish to strike
Sit-In	Workers take over the factory and keep management out

Trade union aims

- Good wages so that workers have a higher standard of living
- Reasonable hours of work with sufficient holidays
- More pay for overtime and piecework
- Benefits for members who are sick, retired or on strike
- Educational schemes, especially for apprentices and young workers
- Control of the supply of labour to maintain employment
- Political action in support of causes in which the union believes
- To give working people a voice on national bodies
- Cooperation with other trade unions
- Participation in talks on the economy with the government and employers

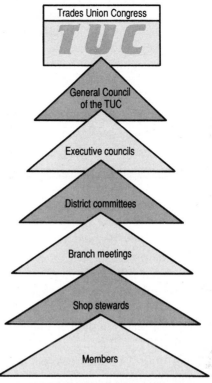

THE SYSTEM OF REPRESENTATION THROUGH TRADES UNIONS

Caterpillar closure would hit 300 other companies

Caterpillar workers may defy court on sit-in

Caterpillar management goes to law

Caterpillar workforce stage sit-in

White-collar staff quit Caterpillar occupation

AEU may order end to sit-in

Caterpillar chief buries hope of plant reprieve

Case Study:
The Caterpillar Occupation

We have seen that the job of the shop steward is to represent the views and opinions of the trade union members in discussion and negotiation with employers.

In 1987 the shop stewards at the Caterpillar works at Tannochside, Uddingston, near Glasgow, were pushed to the forefront of the process of representation when the company announced that it intended to close the plant. The occupation of the plant by the workers which followed this announcement was an important episode in industrial relations in Scotland. For a brief period, the determination of a group of workers to save their jobs attracted widespread support throughout the country.

The Caterpillar Company in Scotland

The Caterpillar Tractor Company was founded in the USA in 1927. At first it made farm equipment, but following World War II it began to concentrate on making heavy, earth-moving equipment. In the 1950s and 1960s the company grew rapidly, opening many overseas manufacturing plants to cope with the increasing worldwide demand for its high-technology products. One of these plants was opened at Tannochside, Uddingston, near Glasgow.

By the early 1980s, however, the company was faced with a number of problems: competition, especially from Japanese manufacturers; the collapse in demand for Caterpillar's products in the Third World because of financial problems in these countries; and a number of political factors which undermined the USA's position in the world market. Between 1982 and 1984 Caterpillar lost over $500 million. Something had to be done.

The company closed four plants in the USA and two in Europe in 1983-84. It also introduced a new programme called 'Plant With A Future' (PWAF) in its remaining factories. This involved a massive reorganisation and investment so that the remaining plants could compete with their Japanese rivals.

19 SEPTEMBER 1986. . . "At a media event held in the Caterpillar factory today it was announced that the Glasgow plant has been selected to build an advanced, high-technology crawler tractor capable of working an 8-hour shift without re-fuelling. Malcolm Rifkind, Secretary of State for Scotland, confirmed that the Government was providing a grant as part of the company's £62.5 million investment plan to re-equip the plant.

The Glasgow plant is a 'Plant With A Future' and the future looks good for the 1200 workers and their families.'

14 JANUARY 1987. . . 'At a press conference held today in the Hospitality Inn, Glasgow, Ken Robinson, the American manager of Caterpillar's Glasgow factory, read out a statement from the Caterpillar management in Peoria, Illinois:
"Caterpillar Corporation said today it plans further consolidation of its manufacturing space as a part of its long-term plans to reduce costs and improve efficiency. . . . The company said it contemplates closing two plants in the United States. Outside the United States, Caterpillar intends to close the 1.1 million square foot Glasgow, Scotland facility."
Over the next 12 to 15 months the plant will gradually be run down and will eventually close.'

The Joint Occupation Committee

The reaction of the Convener of the Tannochside factory's shop stewards, John Brannan, to this remarkable about-turn by the company was short and sharp. He announced:

'On behalf of the hourly paid workers, we are now occupying the plant.'

On 15 January the management of the plant were allowed into the factory to collect any personal belongings. For the next 103 days the workers occupied the plant and the management set up their headquarters in the Hospitality Inn in Glasgow.

Inside the plant, the workers elected a Joint Occupation Committee (JOC) consisting of 22 leading shop stewards representing the five different unions involved in the occupation. These shop stewards represented 800 engineers, 44 electricians and plumbers, 72 workers in the drawing office and planning departments, 140 clerical staff and security officers, and 116 foremen and supervisors - the whole range of 'blue-collar' and 'white-collar' workers employed at the plant.

Convener John Brannan

While some groups of workers were more enthusiastic about the occupation than others, and splits were soon to develop amongst them, the JOC did manage to unite the workforce in a remarkable effort to save the jobs of the 1238 men and women who worked in the Caterpillar plant.

WHAT DID JOC DO TO REPRESENT THE WORKERS?

1. It launched a financial appeal for funds which was remarkably successful. An average of £20 000 a week was collected by the 'U-can-collect' committee. The total amount collected for the fighting fund from all sources was £340 000 – an outstanding achievement.

2. Members of the JOC frequently met with leading politicians including Neil Kinnock, Donald Dewar, Malcolm Rifkind and Conservative MPs and put forward the views of the workers to them. This involved a great amount of time and effort which was not always rewarded with the kind of support the workers hoped for.

3. Lobbying of Parliament was an important aspect of the JOC's work. They were successful in having the occupation brought to the forefront of MPs' attention in debates in the House of Commons.

4. The JOC ensured worldwide publicity for their cause with the building of the 'Pink Panther', a tractor made by workers but painted bright pink rather than the usual yellow of the Caterpillar tractors. The workers wanted the tractor to go to Band Aid, then when the offer was declined plans were made for it to be sent to Nicaragua by the Scottish War on Want charity. Eventually, the tractor stayed in George Square in Glasgow for the rest of the occupation period and was eventually returned to the Caterpillar company. But it had served the purpose of focussing public and media attention on the efforts of the workers.

5. Members of the JOC worked tirelessly to gain the support of Caterpillar workers and union members in Britain, Europe and the USA. Their efforts brought mixed results because many of the workers in Caterpillar's other plants were afraid that they might be next on the closure list. They did succeed in getting support in Illinois from the US workers who wore tartan ribbons on their employee identification badges or attached to their hats. But they were less successful in persuading workers in other Caterpillar plants to support them by boycotting goods (normally made in Glasgow) which the company was now buying from other suppliers.

6. The Committee did have some success in persuading workers other companies and industries to support them. Dockers at Greenock and Grangemouth refused to handle Caterpillar crates, as did workers at a number of transport companies. Shop stewards' committees and mass meetings of workers were addressed by JOC representatives at Jaguar, Peugeot-Talbot, Ferranti, Liverpool docks and many other workplaces, and financial support was given by these workers.

7. Perhaps the greatest show of support for the JOC's efforts came on the 28 February 1987 when 8000 people marched from Uddingston railway station to the plant and attended a demonstration in support of the occupation. The speakers included people representing a wide range of industry, politics, religion and the community. This was a remarkable tribute to the efforts of the workers in general and the JOC in particular.

   Out of this demonstration of support grew the Women's Support Group which became influential in the campaign.

8. When the Caterpillar company eventually decided to go to court to force the workers to end their occupation, the JOC played its part in meeting with Government officials to look at the possible alternatives for the future of the plant under another owner.

   By this stage there were deep divisions within the workforce and the white-collar workers had mostly abandoned the occupation. This highlights how hard the remaining members of the JOC had to work to carry on the fight to save the workers' jobs. To have represented the workers for the 103 days in all the ways mentioned had taken great energy, skill and commitment.

'Pink Panther' in George Square Glasgow

THE CATERPILLAR 'CODE OF WORLDWIDE CONDUCT AND OPERATING PRINCIPLES'

'We intend to hold to a single high standard of integrity everywhere. We will keep our word. We won't promise more than we can reasonably expect to deliver, nor will we make commitments we don't intend to keep. The goal of corporate communication is truth – well and persuasively told.'

I WANT TO GO TO NICARAGUA

The end of the occupation

The occupation of the Caterpillar plant ended on Sunday 26 April, 103 days after it began. In spite of efforts to attract a buyer for the plant, none was found. When it finally closed in October 1987, over 600 workers had no alternative job to go to. They joined the ranks of the unemployed which stood at around 20 per cent of the male population in the area.

Did the shop stewards fail in their job of representing the union members at Caterpillar? Really they had very little chance of success right from the start. The company was determined that it would close the plant at Uddingston and not even the efforts of Malcolm Rifkind, the Secretary of State for Scotland, to persuade the company to change its mind brought any change in its attitude. No doubt the shop stewards made mistakes – this was the first time many of them had been faced with such a situation. Some, like John Brannan, were criticised for pursuing their own personal interests rather than trying to get the best deal for the workers. But Brannan and his colleagues maintained throughout the dispute that what they were doing was fighting to save jobs. In the end it was the determination of the company, and the refusal of the national officers of the unions to continue to support an occupation which had been declared illegal by the courts, that ended this remarkable chapter in Scottish industrial history. The shop stewards on the JOC had fought an impressive fight but the odds were stacked against them all along.

Q UESTIONS

1. What products did Caterpillar make and sell?
2. What problems did the company suffer from in the early 1980s?
3. Describe the actions the company took to solve its problems.
4. Why did the workers at Tannochside decide to occupy the factory?
5. What was JOC?
6. Who did JOC represent?
7. What problems did JOC face?
8. Write a short report describing the main actions taken by JOC to represent the workers at Tannochside.
9. What was the result of the occupation?

A CTIVITIES

Imagine you are a shop steward in a factory which is about to close. Many of the workers are in favour of occupying the factory to prevent losing jobs. You have been asked to write a report for the workforce using the information from the Caterpillar experience, showing the ways in which the occupation was successful and also the problems and difficulties involved. Your report should end with a recommendation to the workers in your own factory on whether or not they should occupy the factory, based on the evidence from the Caterpillar occupation.

Worker representation – *good or bad?*

Many companies consult with union representatives when important decisions are about to be made, but others, like Caterpillar, do not. In recent years a number of companies have made special arrangements with their workers. These include **non-union agreements**, in which the workers agree not to join a trade union in return for higher wages and better working conditions. Many of the Japanese companies which have set up factories in Britain have made such arrangements. The danger for the workers is that when problems arise they do not have the support of the union.

Other companies have entered into **single-union agreements**. This means that all the workers in the factory are allowed to join only one union, with which the management negotiates and discusses working conditions. Companies believe that this is better than trying to negotiate with a number of different unions which might have different ideas, and avoids disagreements. Many trades unions are against this because their members are denied jobs in these factories. In 1988 the Ford Motor Company negotiated a single-union agreement with the Amalgamated Engineering Union (AEU) for a new factory to be opened in Dundee, but pressure from other trades unions forced the agreement to be cancelled and the factory was built abroad.

Other companies take the opposite view and believe in **worker participation**. This means that representatives of the workers are involved in all decisions taken by the Board of Directors and the local management. Some even have schemes for the workers to share some of the profits made by the company. The John Lewis Partnership is an example of a company which gives its employees (or partners as they are called) a say in the running of the company.

1. What is meant by the phrase 'non-union agreement?
2. What is a 'single-union agreement'?
3. What is meant by the phrase 'worker participation'?
4. In which of the three situations described above are workers best represented?

Union strengths and weaknesses

How effective are trades unions in representing their members? The answer to this question depends on many factors, some of which are beyond the control of the unions.

Larger unions usually do better than smaller unions, simply because they have more members and this puts them in a stronger position. In recent years there have been many **amalgamations** in which unions have joined together because 'Unity is Strength'.

But a number of other things will also have an influence on whether or not a union can represent its members effectively. Much depends on the attitude of the employers and whether or not they are prepared to listen to the unions' points of view. A great deal also depends on the attitude of the Government. Since 1979 the Conservative Government has passed a number of laws which have made the unions weaker by restricting their right to picket workplaces, laying down how votes are to be taken, and fining them heavily if the law is broken.

The effectiveness of the trades unions is also dependent on the strength of the economy. If a company is making profits it is more likely to listen to the views of the unions and grant them any reasonable requests. If times are bad and there are no profits and perhaps even the possibility of closure, then the trades unions have to be careful not to make things worse. The level of unemployment is also important, because when unemployment is high (as it has been during the last decade), the employers are in a stronger position. If unions make too many or too great demands on behalf of their members, employers can find replacements from among the unemployed more easily. When unemployment is low and workers are scarce, the unions are in a much better position to represent their members.

Representation in industrial relations - *Simulation Exercise*

For this exercise, you should divide into two groups of 3-6 people, one group to act as the management and the other as the trades union representative from the company's three factories. The exercise is concerned with a meeting between the two groups to discuss the problems of the company and reach a decision about what action should be taken.

The rules of the exercise are as follows:
1. Some time should be spent in preparation for the meeting. This will involve studying all the facts available (all the information is available to both sides). You may also wish to try to decide your group's policy and tactics before entering the meeting with the other group.
2. The Managing Director should open the meeting. (This can be done in several ways – by presenting *all* the alternatives open to management, or by stating the preferred decision and giving reason for this.) The MD should also act as chairperson.
3. A decision *must* be reached.
4. A time-limit of 1hour 15min maximum is recommended, but your teacher will advise you on this.
5. At the end of the exercise there should be some discussion about what happened and why. To help in this, the meeting can be tape-recorded, or the remaining members of the class can act as observers and take notes on what happens during the meeting.

KEYWORDS

The following Keywords are used in this Unit. Make sure you have understood what they mean.

shop steward
industrial relations
negotiations
arbitration
industrial action

non-union agreement
single-union agreement
worker participation
amalgamation

Company Profile DUNEDIN TEXTILES LTD is a long-established company which manufactures woollen jerseys and fashionwear. In recent years the company has suffered from competition both from other UK companies and from foreign companies which can produce the same quality of products at lower prices (mainly because they pay lower wages). In spite of the introduction of the most up-to-date machinery, Dunedin's profits are continuing to fall.

A solution to the company's problems seemed possible when it started selling more products in the USA, but the fall in the value of the dollar against the pound sterling has slowed down this area of growth. The company is now in danger of bankruptcy unless drastic measures are taken soon. A meeting of the management and trades unions representatives from the company's three factories has been called to discuss the possible decisions facing the company and its workers.

NEWSPAPER REPORT. . . . .
Peter Jones, General Secretary of the Textile Workers' Union, speaking today at his union's London headquarters, said, 'We must resist any threat to close down factories because, once closed, they are lost forever.'

TELEVISION NEWS SUMMARY. . . . .
One of Dunedin's leading shareholders said in an off-the-cuff statement today that the only real option open to the company's negotiators going into tomorrow's crucial meeting with the unions was to close one of the factories and protect the jobs of the remaining workers. Any other decision would simply be putting off the evil day and would lead to bigger problems in the future.

DUNEDIN TEXTILES LTD. . . . . (Factfile)

COMPANY PROFITS	
1986:	£2 500 000
1987:	£2 000 000
1988:	£600 000
1989:	£100 000
1990:	−£200 000 (loss)

LOCATION OF FACTORIES

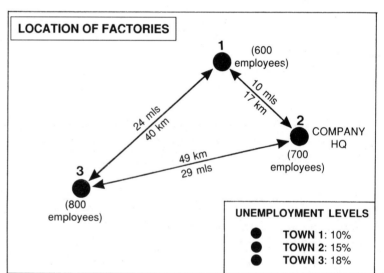

1 (600 employees)
2 COMPANY HQ (700 employees)
3 (800 employees)
10 mls / 17 km
24 mls / 40 km
49 km / 29 mls

UNEMPLOYMENT LEVELS
- **TOWN 1**: 10%
- **TOWN 2**: 15%
- **TOWN 3**: 18%

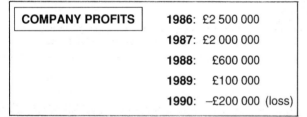

SALES (£m)

20 — 15 — 10 — 5

1980   1985   1990

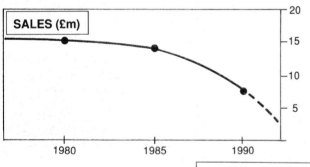

VALUE OF £ AGAINST $

$1.90 — $1.85 — $1.80 — $1.75 — $1.70 — $1.65 — $1.60

1986 1987 1988 1989 1990

BOARD of DIRECTORS' INSTRUCTION TO MANAGEMENT REPRESENTATIVES:

POSSIBLE ACTION:

1. Reduce wages of all workers

2. Introduce part-time working for all workers (1 week on, 1 week off)

3. Close 1 of the 3 factories and make workers redundant to protect jobs of others

RESULTS OF SURVEY OF TRADES UNION MEMBERS

	% FOR	% AGAINST
1. Reduced wages for all	10	90
2. Part-time working for all	20	80
3. Close one factory	30	70

LOCAL AND NATIONAL REPRESENTATION

We saw in Chapter 1, Unit 3, that we elect people to represent us at local, national and international level.

What kinds of people represent us? What should we expect them to do for us? What do they think about the people they represent?

In this Unit we look at a case study of a real Member of Parliament, Henry McLeish MP, who represents the people of Fife Central constituency. This case study will help us to understand more about the meaning of **representation** and answer many of our questions.

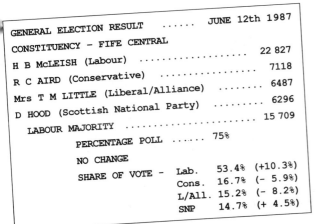

```
GENERAL ELECTION RESULT  ......  JUNE 12th 1987
CONSTITUENCY - FIFE CENTRAL
H B McLEISH (Labour) .................... 22 827
R C AIRD (Conservative) ................ 7118
Mrs T M LITTLE (Liberal/Alliance) ........ 6487
D HOOD (Scottish National Party) ......... 6296
    LABOUR MAJORITY ...................... 15 709
         PERCENTAGE POLL ...... 75%
    NO CHANGE
    SHARE OF VOTE -  Lab.  53.4%  (+10.3%)
                     Cons. 16.7%  (- 5.9%)
                     L/All. 15.2% (- 8.2%)
                     SNP   14.7%  (+ 4.5%)
```

```
PROFILE OF AN M.P.

        NAME:  HENRY B. McLEISH
         AGE:  40
   EDUCATION:  BUCKHAVEN HIGH SCHOOL & HERIOT-WATT
               UNIVERSITY
      FAMILY:  WIFE (MARGARET), SON (NIALL, 14),
               DAUGHTER (CLARE, 12)
 PRESENT JOB:  MEMBER OF PARLIAMENT for FIFE CENTRAL
               CONSTITUENCY.SPONSORED BY NUPE
PREVIOUS JOBS: LOCAL GOVERNMENT COUNCILLOR, PART-TIME
               UNIVERSITY LECTURER, PROFESSIONAL
               FOOTBALLER with EAST FIFE F.C., LEADER
               OF FIFE REGIONAL COUNCIL
   POLITICAL
  EXPERIENCE:  INVOLVED IN LOCAL GOVERNMENT, 1974-1987
BIGGEST POLITICAL
INFLUENCE ON LIFE:  GRANDPARENTS
    AMBITION:  A LABOUR GOVERNMENT! TO ASSIST IN SOME
               WAY IN IMPLEMENTING LABOUR PARTY POLICY
```

An Interview with Henry McLeish MP

Question 1: How did you become an MP?

Answer: In the early 1970s I joined the Labour Party – joining a political party is the first step for most people in becoming an MP. From there I became involved in local government and in the early 1980s I thought that a useful next step would be to become an MP.

That's a difficult thing to achieve. Before the re-selection process starts for an MP you have to do a lot of work, speaking to and influencing people, meeting with trades unions and members of the party, to try to create the idea that you may be a serious candidate for election to Parliament. At the re-selection process itself you are really dependent on the help of the individual members and trades unions to nominate and elect you as the party's candidate for the election.

Question 2: What do you see as the link between your **constituents**, yourself and the decision-making process in Parliament?

Answer: For me, a key issue is the party **manifesto** – a document setting out the party's policies on many things which interest people. During the election this is discussed both nationally and locally. You are giving to people the ideas which you can be associated with.

The first link, then, is that we put forward ideas, then the voters elect me to work in Parliament to try to implement them.

The second link is my ability to reflect in Parliament the kind of community I live in, the kinds of problems we experience, and to raise issues in Parliament which affect individuals within the **constituency**.

Thirdly, there is a debate about the remoteness of Parliament, and increasingly a debate about how remote it is in relation to Scottish interests and issues. One of my key jobs is to look at the links that exist between the constituency, the people and Parliament and to make sure at every turn that I am their link.

If you can achieve all of these things you retain the confidence of the people you represent.

Question 3: How important is it to you that you represent your constituents' views when you vote in the House of Commons?

Answer: There is always a danger that you slavishly follow every single aspect of your manifesto when it could conflict with the interests of your constituency.

If it is a matter of conscience, e.g. the abortion issue, I must be in tune with the people I represent. At the end of the day I make an independent judgment on these matters, but that is one area where the manifesto has to come second to the views of constituents. I think it is vitally important that I continue to represent the interests of my constituents even though they may conflict with a commitment to the party's programme.

Question 4: Apart from your constituents' views, do any other factors influence how you vote in Parliament?

Answer: I don't think so.

Two key issues influence the voting patterns of the House of Commons. One is the party policy and the **Whip system**. The bulk of the voting is decided prior to the MP attending the House.

The second key area involves individual issues, e.g. official secrets, abortion, experiments on animals. All of these are issues on which the Labour Party has a view but not necessarily a definite policy, and these are the issues where I can have some discretion as to how I vote. These will normally reflect my personal beliefs, but also how strong that particular issue is in the constituency.

There are pressure groups for every possible activity under the sun. That is healthy and good for **democracy**, but the work of these groups does not influence how I vote. What is important is that they educate the MP on a whole range of very complex issues that he or she could be ignorant of. They educate, but very rarely do they change opinion.

Secondly, I'm back in my constituency as often as possible. I meet groups, speak to people and hold surgeries, and as a result have my finger on the pulse of the constituency. I'm not remote. My wife and my secretary also keep my feet on the ground and let me know quickly of any concern or interest within the constituency.

I have a permanent office in the constituency, with a full-time secretary five days a week and an Answer-phone service. Constituents can also write either to London or to the local office. Finally, my telephone number is in the directory and people can contact me at home.

Question 6: At the last General Election, 22 827 people voted for you, but 19 901 voted for one of the other candidates.

Does it make any difference to you when you are representing constituents that they voted for someone else, and how do you find out their views and opinions?

Answer: No, there is no difference, and that is absolutely vital because it is the essence of democracy. Before the election, in the three weeks' campaign, you are there appealing to Labour voters because that's your party, and hoping to attract some other people.

When the Returning Officer announces that you have been elected, every elector in the constituency is on the same level. I know many people in my area who are SNP or Conservative Party supporters, but I make no distinction. Finding out their views is reasonably

straightforward. I do not try to push Labour Party policies down people's throats every time I speak. There is a commonsense approach as an MP – if people have a concern they can bring it forward whether or not they like me or the Labour Party.

Question 7: How important is it that people should use their right to vote?

Answer: It is very important. In the UK we have a compulsory system of registration which means that some 90 per cent of the population is registered as being eligible to vote. It is vital that people use their vote. It is vital that people use their vote because (a) I am opposed to 'armchair critics' – people who complain but haven't taken the trouble to vote, not only for me but for any candidate; (b) a democracy is only as strong as those who participate in it – it's more than MPs or councillors, it's the people. An educated democracy will use their votes because they have views and ideas which they want to be reflected; (c) in some areas like Scotland and Wales there is a danger that people won't use their vote because it never seems to make an impact on the type of Government they get. Nevertheless, its absolutely crucial and its something I would always encourage even though it might be against me.

Question 8: What kinds of issues do your constituents ask for your help on?

Answer: In common with most MPs throughout the country, I deal with more housing issues than anything else – housing benefit, repairs, or people seeking a house.

Secondly, social security which has become so complicated now that people have great difficulty understanding the system.

Thirdly, the question of unemployment is still a major issue. It's one that I can't do much about, except counsel people and help them with advice about benefits.

Fourthly, there is a whole range of legal matters about divorce, legal aid, etc. A lot of elderly people and pensioners come to me with housing and social security problems.

Question 9: Do you feel that constituents are adequately and effectively represented in the decision-making process?

Answer: They can never be adequately represented in any decision-making process. But in Central Fife, people get a reasonable return for their investment in their councillors and MP. Some weeks I really don't have the time to go to London - I could spend seven days a week dealing with problems in Fife, but I have to go to London for three or four days.

Compared with the US Congress, the support staff we get is an absolute disgrace, a joke. We could do much more if we had more support staff. But if the MP or councillor is committed, people can come to them and enjoy a reasonable level of success.

Note to the teacher: the questions provided for this section should not be seen as the only method of using this extensive and sometimes difficult resource. It may be useful to highlight appropriate individual questions and answers when considering other areas of the syllabus rather than considering the interview as a whole to be tackled at one time.

Q UESTIONS

1. In what ways can the constituents make their views known to the MP? (Ref. Q5 & Q6)

2. What kinds of problems do people take to the MP? (Ref. Q8)

3. Why is the MP not always successful in representing the constituents? (Ref Q9)

4. Why is it important that people should use their right to vote in elections? (Ref. Q7)

5. How important does the MP consider it that he should represent his constituents? (Ref Q3 & Q6)

6. In what three ways is the MP a link between constituents and the decision-making process? (Ref. Q2)

Rights, duties and responsibilites

In the interview with Henry McLeish, MP the **rights**, **duties** and **responsibilities** of the Member of Parliament and the electors were mentioned several times. Perhaps the most important duty that electors have is that they should actually use their vote in elections. People who do not vote really can have no reason to complain if decisions are made with which they disagree. They also have certain rights, especially the right to expect that their MP will represent them to the best of his or her abilities and will try to help them if they have a problem.

The fact that each elector and each MP has both rights and responsibilities is important because they depend upon each other. The MP must try to earn the respect and trust of his or her constituents. The constituents have to be reasonable in expectations of the demands on their MP, otherwise a great deal of time can be wasted in looking into problems which the MP will never be able to help with. This is an example of how people have to cooperate with each other in order to achieve the best results for everyone.

Representation in action

In November 1988, Jim Sillars of the SNP won a remarkable victory in a by-election in the Glasgow Govan constituency. He overturned a Labour majority at the General Election of over 19 500 and emerged with a majority of 3554. His first announcement as the newly elected MP showed that he intended to represent the views of his constituents right from the start. (See extract, bottom right of page.)

Jim Sillars, MP

THE RESULT

Sillars, Jim (Scottish National Party)	**14,677**
Gillespie, Bob (Labour)	11,123
Hamilton, Graeme (Conservative)	2,207
Ponsonby, Bernard (Democrat)	1,246
Campbell, George (Green)	345
Chalmers, Douglas (Communist)	281
Sutch, David (Monster Raving Loony)	174
Clark, Fraser (Rainbow Alliance)	51
SNP majority	3,554

Percentage share of vote: SNP 48 per cent, Lab 36, Con 7.3, Dem 4.1, Others 2.8.
Lost deposits: Democrat, Green, Comm, MR Loony, R Alliance
Swing to SNP: 33.1
Percentage poll 60.2 per cent.

General Election, June, 1987: Bruce Millan, (Lab) 24,071 (64.8); Alasdair Ferguson, SDP/Liberal Alliance, 4,562 (12.3); Janet Girsman, Conservative, 4,411 (11.9); Felix McCabe, Scottish National Party, 3,851 (10.4); Douglas Chalmers, Communist, 237 (0.6). Labour majority 19,509. Turnout 72.6 per cent.

(source: *The Scotsman*, 11 November, 1988)

The new MP for Govan said his first act as elected representative was to telephone Strathclyde's chief constable, Mr Andrew Sloan, to arrange a meeting over the rising crime rate in the constituency, particularly drug abuse.

He had been concerned by reports from the people of Govan that they had reported the names and addresses of known drug pushers to the police and no action had been taken.

"This is one area we must clear up," said Mr Sillars. "There have been allegations made by the local community that they have been able to identify pushers and no notice has been taken by the police. It is my duty to go to the chief constable and say the community has said this and ask what is his reply."

(source: *The Scotsman*, 12 November 1988.)

Make sure your voice is heard!

The job of an elected councillor or MP is to represent people. But you cannot be represented properly unless you make your views and opinions known. Here are some ways in which you can do this:

QUESTION

Which of these do you think is the most effective way of influencing an elected representative?

Give a reason for your answer.

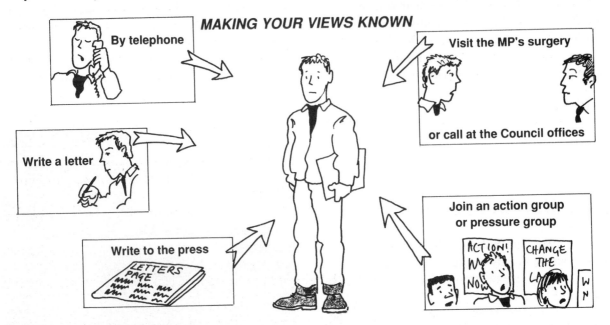

MAKING YOUR VIEWS KNOWN

The diagram above shows some of the ways in which people can try to influence their councillor or MP. But remember that there are many influences at work on representatives and they have to consider the issues carefully before making a decision. Look again at the answers which were given to Questions 3 and 4 by Henry McLeish MP.

QUESTION

List in order of importance what you think should be the three most important influences on an MP's decisions. Say why you think they are important.

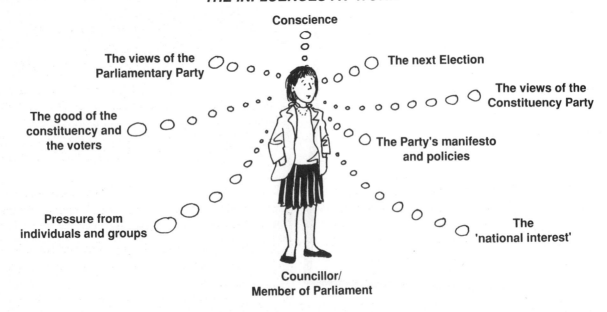

THE INFLUENCES AT WORK

'PLANS FOR NUCLEAR FLIGHTS FROM WESTFORD'

Background

Westford is a town of 13 000 people in south-west Scotland. It relies for its prosperity on the summer visitors who come to the area to enjoy the nearby beaches, golf courses and leisure and entertainment facilities. For a number of years the number of summer visitors has been falling as more people prefer to go abroad in search of the sun.

Westford Airport lies close to the town. It is especially busy in the summer because it is the main airport for people flying to Canada and the USA from Scotland. The airport has an advantage over the airports in Glasgow and Edinburgh because it is very rarely closed as a result of poor weather conditions like fog or snow.

Its biggest disadvantage is that it is too far from the big populations of Glasgow and Edinburgh to be attractive to the airlines flying the highly profitable routes between Scotland and London. If Westford Airport lost its transatlantic flights to these other airports it might be in danger of closing.

About 50 kilometres to the south of Westford, just over the English border, there is a nuclear power station. Attached to it is a plant which can re-process plutonium, a nuclear fuel which can be used in nuclear power stations and in making nuclear weapons.

The company which owns the plant has recently won a contract to export re-processed plutonium to Japan and would like to fly this product out from Westford Airport.

The people of Westford have formed a protest group to campaign against the company's proposal. It is thought that about 90 per cent of the local people are opposed to the plan.

Leaflet from protest group

For and against

Press Interview with Managing Director

'Westford Airport would be ideal for us. It is situated close to the power plant and is open all year round. Our flights would be as safe as any other flights and should present no problems to the local community. The benefits to the people of Westford would be that the jobs of those working at the airport would be guaranteed because the airport would not be in danger of closing as long as our flights to Japan continue. There might even be some additional jobs. This would benefit the whole town.'

OPPOSE NUCLEAR FLIGHTS

Help us to campaign against these flights because –
- They are dangerous
- They will cause unnecessary disturbance
- They will affect our holiday trade
- They will not benefit the local community
- They can never be 100% safe

YOU can help by protesting to your local councillor and Member of Parliament

Statement by airport trade-union representative

'This contract could guarantee the long-term future of the airport and with it the jobs of the workers. Remember that these workers spend their wages in the shops and hotels and on entertainment in the town. If we oppose this proposal, the whole town will suffer.'

Statement by local Hotel Owners' Association

'We are opposed to this idea not only because of the obvious dangers involved, but because of the effect it would have on business in the town. If summer visitors stop coming to the area then everyone will suffer as hotels close and people lose their jobs.'

QUESTIONS

1. What can the members of the protest group do to make sure that their councillors and MP know how they feel about the plan?

2. What actions can be taken by the councillors and MP in representing the views of the people of the town?

1. Imagine you are the local MP. You have been invited to a meeting with the company's directors to discuss the issue. Write out a Plan of Action containing all the points you would want to put at the meeting.

Remember your job is to represent your constituents, but there may be other factors which you want to take into account.

Your local area can be an important source if information about representation – how people are represented and how representatives do their jobs. The following activities are designed to help you put into practice in your own area some of the things you have learned about representation.

2. Design a questionnaire containing the questions you would like to ask a local councillor or MP. You can use the interview in this Unit as a model, but you may want to ask different questions about issues in the local area. It could be useful to ask some of the same questions, then compare the answers with those given by Henry McLeish MP.

3. A group from the class should write to a local elected representative, enclosing a copy of the questionnaire and asking if the councillor or MP would consider answering it. This can be done in two ways: either invite the person to send a written reply; or invite him or her to come to the school to meet with your class.

Your teacher will advise you on how to do this. Remember that elected representatives are very busy people.

4. Select a local issue or problem which is receiving attention in the newspapers. Collect cuttings of statements made by the people involved, particularly councillors, and make a wall display or cuttings diary showing how they represent local people's views.

5. Arrange a visit for a small group from the class to meet with a local councillor at the District or Regional Council offices. If you are lucky the councillor may be able to arrange for you to attend a council meeting or a meeting of one of the council's committees so that you can see representation in action. Your teacher will advise you on how to write a letter asking for a visit.

KEYWORDS

The following Keywords are used in this Unit. Make sure you have understood what they mean.

representation	whip system
constituent	democracy
manifesto	proportional representation
constituency	rights duties
	responsibilities

WHAT ABOUT ME?

Listen to me

"I voted for the SNP. I think the only way Scotland will ever be well off is when we run things for ourselves. Scotland in Europe, that's what I want. What did they call all these Labour MP's–the 'feeble fifty'? Well, we'll show them!"

Scottish Nationalist

"The head listens to what we say on Student Council but it never really changes anything, unless he wants to make the change anyway. Like when we wanted social areas for every year. He just said, 'No! No! That would never work. Too many problems'."

School pupil

"We have had women in Parliament for 70 years now and a woman Prime Minister but it's still hard to be selected as a candidate. A woman always has to work twice as hard to get the same job as a man."

Woman

"I think the Government's doing a good job. Look at how prosperous the country has become. I know that it is mainly in the South but given time it will spread all over the country. Up here, though, nobody agrees with me. They all vote Labour and do not care about small businesses."

"Even when we do have Black MPs and councillors the papers say that they are extremists, 'loony left' and all that rubbish."

Shopkeeper

Black

QUESTIONS

1. Which of the people in the cases above are unrepresented because of our electoral system?

2. Which of the people in the cases above are unrepresented because of problems in our society?

3. Given the cases you have read about, write out a list of people who you think do have power in our society.

4. From amongst the cases you have read about, choose one statement you agree with and one statement that you disagree with. Write a sentence giving reasons for your choice.

ACTIVITIES

1. In your groups read through all the statements. You could read them out aloud around your group. Discuss the reasons why these people feel they are unrepresented.

2. Try to think of other situations where people's views are unrepresented.

3. Make a collection of newspaper cuttings which show the views of people who are unrepresented. You could write a report about this in your groups.

An unfair system?

Some people think our system of elections is unfair. This is particularly true of the smaller political parties who feel they would benefit from a system of **proportional representation**. However, not everyone agrees about which PR method would be best.

There are several different systems which might be used but even then they might leave some people unrepresented. (See page 22.)

There are also groups in society who are not represented in Parliament as they should be. The most obvious examples of this are women and ethnic minorities.

If we look at the population of the country you can see that there are slightly more women than men, and that ethnic minorities make up about 4.5 per cent of the population as a whole.

In Parliament, though, the picture looks very different.

UK population, 1986

Males	Females
27.6 million	29.1 million
49%	51%

(source: *Social Trends*, 1988 Reproduced with the permission of the Controller of HMSO.)

UK population and ethnic minorities

	Millions	%
UK population	56.7	100
All ethnic minorities	2.5	4.5
Caribbean	0.5	
Pakistani	0.4	
Bangladeshi	0.1	
Chinese	0.1	
African	0.1	
Others	0.4	

House of Commons and the 'Representative' House (seats)

	1987 election	'Representative' House
Men	609	318
Women	41	332
Black MPs	4	29

(source: *Social Studies Review*, Vol. 3, No. 1.)

Let's look at this situation more closely. If women and ethnic minorities are not properly represented in Parliament it must mean that some other groups are over-represented. In fact, not only is Parliament made up mainly of white males, but of men from a particular kind of background. These tend to be from the traditionally powerful groups in society, the universities, public schools and big business.

Perhaps things are changing, though?

Q UESTIONS

1. Make up a table which puts together the information on population and representation in Parliament.

UK population	% Population	MPs, 1987 Election	Representative House
Men			
Women			
Ethnic minorities			

2. Give one reason why this situation could be said to be unfair.

Female candidates and MPs for the three main parties 1974-87

	All Women[a]		Conservative		Labour		Alliance[b]	
	Candidates	MPs	Candidates	MPs	Candidates	MPs	Candidates	MPs
Feb 1974	143	23	33	9	40	13	40	0
Oct 1974	161	27	30	7	50	18	49	0
1979	210	19	31	8	52	11	51	0
1983	255	23[c]	37	13	77	10	71	0
1987	325	41	46	17	92	21	105	2

Notes: (a) includes females elected or standing for other parties, e.g. in 1987 one female SNP MP was returned: (b) Liberal Party 1974-79: (c) excludes five women elected in by-elections: 2 Labour; 2 Alliance; 1 Conservative.

(source: *Social Studies Review*, Vol. 3, No. 1.)

Record number of women

Only a strong surge to Labour would hav significantly increased the number of wome elected. It has 21 women members, compare with 17 for the Tories, two for the Alliance an one Scottish Nationalist, making up 6.3 per cer of elected members.

The 300 Group, which campaigns across party divides to get more women in Parliament described the result as a great victory for women. "The figures have been drifting up and down over the years, but this time we have really broken through."

(source: *The Independent*, 13 June 1987.)

The 300 Group, the all-party campaign for more women MPs, will undoubtedly be disappointed by the continual slow rise in the number of women in the House since the war. The group looks a very long way from its target of having 300 women in Parliament before the end of the century. The election result has at least brought the return of a woman Prime Minister and more women into ministerial office. Some women might argue, however, that the Ministry for Women, promised by Labour if it was elected, might have been more effective in the long term in boosting the number of female candidates and MPs.

(source: *Social Studies Review*, Vol. 3, No. 1.)

Black candidates and their performance in the 1987 election

		% of vote behind winner or in front of 2nd placed candidate	Swing (%)
Conservative (6)			
Raj Chandran	Preston	-24.0	4.5 to Lab
Nirj Deva	Hammersmith	- 6.9	4.5 to Lab
Nazir Khan	Birmingham Sparkbrook	-35.1	1.6 to Lab
Kristian Nath	Manchester Blackley	-19.1	4.1 to Lab
Paul Dischal	Birmingham Small Heath	-45.2	1.5 to Lab
John Taylor	Birmingham Perry Barr	-13.5	0.4 to Lab
Labour (14)			
Diane Abbott*	Hackney N.	+19.8	1.8 to Con
Vidya Anand	Folkestone	-48.0	0.5 to Con
Mohammed Aslom	Nottingham E.	- 1.0	1.5 to Lab
Paul Boateng*	Brent S.	+19.5	3.4 to Con
Ben Bousquet	Kensington	-11.0	1.1 to Lab
Bernie Grant*	Tottenham	+ 8.2	6.8 to Con
Najma Hafeez	Stafford	-24.3	1.2 to Con
Ashak Patel	Eastbourne	-51.1	0.5 to Lab
Praful Patel	Brent N.	-35.1	0.9 to Con
Russel Profitt	Lewisham E.	-11.0	3.2 to Con
Cris St. Hill	Mid-Staffs	-25.9	1.9 to Lab
Mukesh Savani	Sheff. Hallam	-25.9	2.5 to Lab
Keith Vaz*	Leicester E.	+ 3.7	2.8 to Lab
Valerie Vaz	Twickenham	-43.5	0.3 to Con

		% of vote behind winner or in front of 2nd placed candidate	Swing (%)
Alliance (7)			
Mohammed Ali	Blackburn	-39.9	4.8 to Lab
Balder Chahal	Liverpool Riverside	-62.0	5.5 to Lab
Sumal Fernando	Notts. N.	-33.2	7.0 to Lab
Zerbano Gifford	Harrow E.	-32.0	6.7 to Lab
Lutfe Kamal	Wakefield	-34.5	13.8 to Lab
Manzoor Moghal	Bradford W.	-40.5	8.9 to Lab
Gurdial Sangha	Birmingham, Ladywood	-48.4	

Note: * Elected.

(source: *Social Studies Review*, Vol. 3, No. 1.)

Voting intentions of ethnic minorities 1983/87 (%)

	Asians		Afro-Caribbeans	
	1983 poll	1987 poll	1983 poll	1987 poll
Con	9	23	7	6
Lab	81	67	88	86
Alliance	9	10	5	7
Swing	14% to Con		0.5% to Con	

(source: *The Guardian*, 19 June 1987.)

Q UESTIONS

1. Draw a simple graph and describe the trend of the graph for the following:

   a) The number of women MPs since February 1974.

   b) The number of women candidates since February 1974.

2. What conclusion do you draw from comparing the two graphs?

3. Which political party gives the best opportunity for women candidates?

   Give reasons for your answer (see table bottom left on p. 44).

4. What is The 300 Group?

5. Is the result of the election, 'A great victory for women', or should they be, 'disappointed by the continual slow rise in the number of women in the House'?

6. How many of the Black candidates had any real chance of winning? Look at the table above top and pick out the ones who were close to winning.

7. Why do you think so many ethnic minority voters support the Labour party?

8. What changes can you see between the election results in 1983 and 1987 as far as women and ethnic minorities are concerned?

Women in Parliament – why so few?

It is obvious that this issue is more complicated than it first appears to be.

- Women are only just beginning to break down traditional barriers which have kept them out of positions of power in society.
- Women still bear most of the responsibilities for their families. The House of Commons works unusual hours which don't suit the majority of women who have family responsibilities.
- Women are often not selected as candidates because those who select them are mostly male and fear that a woman candidate might lose votes.
- There is still a great deal of **prejudice** in our society against women.

Ethnic minority representatives – why so few?

- The ethnic minority population is concentrated in certain parts of the country. In other places the prejudice against a Black candidate would be seen as a vote loser for the Party.
- There is still a great deal of racial prejudice in our society.

Here are some other factors which you should study and take into account before completing the Activities in this unit.

Racism is the shame of Scotland

The Scottish Ethnic Minority Research Unit has reported that there is "a climate of racism" in Scotland. They add:
"The belief that Scotland has better race relations than any other part of Britain is a myth."
More than 80 per cent of Asians have experienced some form of racial harassment.
There is a growing dossier of Asian families persecuted by neighbours on housing estates – bricks through windows, break-ins, excrement through letter-boxes, the whole depressing gamut of neighbourhood Nazism....
We're kidding ourselves if we believe Scots aren't racist.
No nation is more nationalistic than Scotland – ask any unfortunate Englishman.
Maybe some of us can't accept that we're a multi-racial nation now.
Whatever happened to that splendid old Scots saying: "We're a' Jock Tamson's bairns"? (**Tom Brown**)

(source: *The Daily Record*, 25 April 1988.)

Racial offences on increase in Lothian, says report

By BRYAN CHRISTIE

ETHNIC minorities in Lothian are continuing to be subjected to "a steady and seemingly relentless increase in racially motivated abuse and offences," says the region's Community Relations Council....
"In a multi-racial community, the police, who are charged with enforcing the law, must be representative of all sections of the community. We would therefore welcome more inquiries from men and women of the ethnic groups to join the police."
Such a commitment was welcomed by the CRC's senior community relations officer, Mrs Saroj Lal, who said that there were still very few black people employed in the public sector. Both Lothian Region and Edinburgh District councils had expressed their commitment to equal opportunities on paper but that still to be translated into practical job opportunities.

(source: *The Scotsman*, 26 October 1988.)

Problems women face

Women face a number of barriers that slow down their economic advancement.
Education   Only 39 per cent of university students are women – it is difficult to attract women into maths, physics, engineering and technology because these are often stereotyped as being 'not subjects for girls'.
Employment   Many recruitment procedures discriminate informally against women.
Home Work   The division of labour within the home assumes that the male goes out to work. This denies the benefits of joint incomes and joint satisfaction. If both male and female within the household went out to work then this would require a greater amount of flexibility in household organisation.

(source: *Social Studies Review*, Vol. 4, No. 2.)

A CTIVITIES

1. Your class can carry out a **survey** amongst one of the groups that feels unrepresented. Each person interviews several people and the class adds the results together. Use a tally sheet to collect your answers. An example of a tally sheet is given.

You will need to work out your questions in advance so spend some time doing this. Make sure that your questions are clear.

The questions you use will depend on which group you are surveying. (If you are surveying workers you might ask questions about their representation at their work place, rather than in Parliament.)

2. Each member of the class should choose one person to **interview** about how they feel their views are represented in Parliament. You might choose an Asian shop keeper, an unemployed person, or a supporter of one of the political parties.

An interview can be longer than a questionnaire but again you must make up your questions in advance. If your interviewee is similar to one of the people who commented on page 43, are her or his views similar too? If not, how do they differ?

3. Investigate the representation of special groups in your area. The possibilities will vary in different parts of the country.

In the cities – ethnic minorities
 – disabled people
 – elderly people

In the country or smaller towns
 – farmers or farm workers
 – landowners
 – Gaelic speakers

Anywhere – women
 – the political parties
 – unemployed people

You may find that there are organisations which try to represent the interests of these groups. We'll be looking at this in much more detail in Chapter 3 but perhaps your Regional Council or library has information.

KEYWORDS

The following Keywords are used in this Unit. Make sure you have understood what they mean.

electoral system	prejudice
ethnic minorities	survey
	tally sheet

TALLY SHEET

There are 650 Members of Parliament

1. How many women MP's are there?
 about 40 _____
 about 100 _____
 about 300 _____

2. There should be more women MP's
 Agree _____
 Disagree _____

3. Do you think women's views are properly represented in your local area?
 Yes _____
 No _____

Representation?

For many years people have been concerned that although we elect MPs and councillors who work very hard on our behalf it is not just women, ethnic minorities, the unemployed or the Scots who are unrepresented but in fact all of us. Surveys like the one below have been carried out on many occasions.

Question: *How much do you trust a British government of any party to place the needs of this country above the interests of their own political party?*

	%
Just about always	5
Most of the time	34
Only some of the time	46
Almost never	11
Don't know/can't say	4

(source: *British Social Attitudes*. The 1987 Report.)

In another survey over 60 per cent of people said, "people like me do not have any say about what the government does," and 80 per cent agreed that, "all candidates sound good in speeches but you can never tell what they will do after they are elected."
It may seem that we do not think much of the way we are represented but that does not mean that we do not believe in the entire system.

A CTIVITIES

1. Repeat the survey above in your own area.

2. Record the results in the form of a series of pie charts.

3. Compare your results with those from the national survey.

4. Write a brief report which sums up your findings.

3

THE POLITICAL PROCESS

UNIT
3.1

THE DECISION IS...

———————————— (A short play in one scene) ————————————

*The first meeting of the Craigford School Pupils'
Representative Council has been organised. The
Headteacher has asked each year group to vote for two
pupils from that year group to put forward views at the
meeting. In this way each year in the school will have
two representatives at the meeting.*

*Karen and Alex, along with four other third-year
pupils, said they would like to attend the meeting as
third-year representatives. Third-year pupils were
asked to vote to decide which two of these six
candidates would be the representatives. After the
voting, Karen and Alex had most votes so they were
elected as representatives.*

Characters

The Headteacher
Third-year representatives: Karen, Alex
Fourth-year representatives: Craig, Salim
Sixth-year representatives: Paul, Suzanne
Other representatives from other years

(The characters sit round an oval table.)

Headteacher "I would like to welcome all of you to this the first
meeting of the Craigford School Pupils' Representative
Council. As you know, I have called this meeting so
that the views of the pupils in the school can be put
forward and discussed. Maybe some of the **decisions**
taken here will help in the running of the school.
I shall act as **Chairperson** for the meetings. As
chairperson, I decide whose turn it is to speak, and how
long each person can talk. Our first task is to appoint a
Secretary whose job it will be to write down the main
points of the meeting (the **Minutes**). This is the first
item on the **Agenda**.
Any volunteers for the job of Secretary?"

Paul "I propose Suzanne as Secretary. She keeps good, clear
notes of the Hockey Club meetings."

Karen "I agree with that!"

MEETING
CRAIGFORD HIGH SCHOOL
PUPILS' REPRESENTATIVE
COUNCIL
ON 9. 10. 90
AT 3 PM
IN THE LIBRARY

AGENDA:-

1. INTRODUCTIONS.

2. APPOINTMENT OF SECRETARY.

3. LUNCH QUEUES.

4. A.O.C.B

Headteacher	"Any other **nominations**?" (*Pause*) "No? Then Suzanne, are you prepared to be Secretary?"
Suzanne	"Yes. I'll do it."
Headteacher	"Good! Now, the next item on the Agenda is Lunch Queues. This has been raised by Third-year, so Karen or Alex, would you like to start off."
Karen	"We don't think people should be able to jump the queue just because they say they have a meeting to attend. Nobody knows whether they have a meeting or not! Anyway, it should be first there, first served."
Paul	"It isn't first there, first served now. There is a class rota at lunch time so each class has a turn at being first in the queue."
Alex	"Yes, but Karen means the first class should go in first. There should not be other people getting in first."
Craig	"But some meetings are held at lunch-time and if you don't go in early for lunch then you miss the meeting."
Headteacher	"Yes. I can see there is a problem. Now, Karen has suggested there should be no alterations to the published weekly dinner rota. Craig says this is difficult for people with meetings to attend at lunch-time. Any other views about what can be done to solve this problem?"
Paul	"I think we should keep to the class rota system. Then everyone knows where they are!"
Suzanne	"If those who had to attend meetings had to bring a note from the teacher organising the meeting, then others in the queue would know they were being allowed in for a good reason."
Salim	"But who would check on these notes?"
Suzanne	"The person in charge of the queue could check these notes, and those with signed notes could get in early."
Karen	"But there might be dozens!"
Alex	"No. There are not all that many meetings. Anyway not everyone takes school lunch!"
Headteacher	"We now have two suggestions. One is to keep the queues as they are, the other is to allow in early those with notes. Karen, what do you think of this second suggestion?"

Karen	"Well! It might work if there were only a few people each day."
Headteacher	"Any other views?"
	(*Pause*) "Is everyone agreed we should try this second way or do we need a vote?"
Alex	"We could give it a trial run for two or three weeks."
Headteacher	"Does anyone disagree with that suggestion?"
	(*No comments*)
	"The **unanimous** decision of the meeting then is that the lunch queue rota should stay but, for a trial time, those pupils with official signed notes will be able to go in early. Suzanne, have you got that noted?"
Suzanne	"Yes. It is in the Minutes. I'll get them typed and duplicated so that everyone here will have a copy."
Headteacher	"This decision will now be put to other meetings in the school – the House Staff, and the School Board of Management. If they agree, then the decision can be put into action fairly soon. (*Pause*)
	Is there any other business? (*Pause*)
	No, then thank you all for attending. The next meeting will be in three weeks' time."

THE NEXT MEETING WILL BE IN THREE WEEKS TIME.

QUESTIONS

1. In what way are the views of school pupils represented at the meeting?
2. What is the job, at the meeting, of
   a) the Chairperson and b) the Secretary.
3. What are the Minutes of a meeting, and why are they important?
4. Why was a vote not required at this meeting?
5. What was the final decision of the meeting?
6. Who else would be consulted before the final decision would be taken?
7. Why do you think these other groups were to be consulted before a final decision could be made?
8. What would be the responsibilities of the year representatives after the meeting?
9. Find out, using a dictionary, and note the exact meanings of the words in **bold** type in the play.

ACTIVITIES

1. Form into groups of about four, and discuss how the decision was made.
2. Discuss and list what *other* decisions might have been made at the meeting.
3. Discuss and list other *ways* in which the decision at the meeting might have been made.
4. Find out the different types of meetings held in your school.
5. Choose one issue in your school. Organise a meeting (your group) to discuss and reach a decision.

KEYWORDS

The following Keywords are used in this Unit. Make sure you have understood what they mean.

chairperson	agenda	nomination
secretary	decision	unanimous
Minutes		

THE EVENING COURIER

Public Outcry at 'Green Belt' Violation

A storm of protest greeted yesterday's announcement that property developers had applied for planning permission to build two new executive housing estates in the 'Green Belt' area. Two sites have been earmarked – one just south of the Gylefield housing estate and the other to the north-west of the Pentmuir Estate. Both sites lie on the fringe of the Pentmuir Country Park. Concern has already arisen over this whole area with the new building of a supermarket. Residents in the Pentmuir and Gylefield Estates have already formed action groups as rumours of this development have been circulating for several months now. Conservation groups and the Pentmuir Country Park Action Group have vigorously opposed any threat to the Green Belt area. Mr James Bourne, Secretary of the P.C.P.A.G. complained bitterly last night that 'this could be the thin end of the wedge. This is only a small section of the Country Park but who knows where the next development will threaten? We need our country-side. The Pentmuir area is playing an increasingly important role in our residents' leisure time.'

Mr Angus Gordon, on behalf of the Property Developers, issued a statement that the town had long outgrown its boundaries which were in need of being re-drawn. He said 'The town is growing fast. Business and industry is being attracted. We need to build houses to cater for the business community.'

This issue is bound to create a political storm for the local District Council. The Conservative Group are very keen to see a new housing development being built to ease the housing shortage in the more expensive end of the housing market. The Labour Party would much rather see the central area of the town being re-developed.

James Bourne predicted that those opposed to the development would fight all the way demanding a Planning Enquiry if the Council gives the scheme the go-ahead.

The Council decision

Background information

The District Council consists of twenty Councillors. There are twelve Conservative councillors, six Labour councillors, one SNP and one Social and Liberal Democrat. The Conservatives have a majority on the Council, however, on the issue of the new **housing development** there are divisions within the Conservative Group. Nine of the Conservative Group wish to approve **planning permission** for the new development. Led by Group leader Councillor Sheila Thomson, they argue that the town's economy is beginning to grow, especially in the areas of insurance and electronics which are being attracted to the industrial estate. Two new high-quality executive housing areas, in a lovely suburban location at the foot of the Pentmuir Hills with good access to the main town by-pass road, will help to attract new business to the town.
Three Conservative councillors might oppose the scheme, either in its entirety or parts of it.

John MacDonald (Conservative) is a local farmer and a keen lover of the country. He is a member of the Royal Society for the Protection of Birds and works on a voluntary basis as a Ranger in the Country Park, taking groups on hill-walks and nature rambles. He is very concerned about any development outwith the town boundary. The Pentmuir Country Park Action Group expect him to support them.

Alexa Hamilton is the local councillor for the Pentmuir Ward. She has received a great deal of mail from her constituents, protesting against the proposed development. At the last election she had only a very **narrow majority** over her Labour rival. She has in the past supported the building of the new by-pass road and the new supermarket, both of which had mixed support in her ward. She is believed to be in favour of the housing developments and feels that the new residents would probably vote Conservative.

James Millar's constituency contains the smaller – but highly exclusive – Gylefield Estate, some of the wealthiest housing in the town. James Millar (Conservative) has a **safe majority**. He is aware that any extension to the Gylefield Estate would be highly unpopular with the residents there, but the other areas in his Ward are less concerned about the development. Mr Millar owns a growing business and knows how attractive a new housing development would be. He might oppose the development next to the Gylefield Estate but support the one next to the Pentmuir Estate.

The Labour Group oppose the proposed housing developments. They argue that there has been too much new development on the west side of the town and that the central and older, more industrialised areas need to be re-developed. They want to see the older houses renovated and new shopping and leisure facilities built. Leading spokesperson for the Labour Group is **Andrew Weir**, Councillor for the Marston Ward. The Marston area contains some of the town's worst housing. It has suffered greatly from the closure, five years ago, of the nearby engineering works. Mr Weir would like to see the Council directing itself to encouraging new housing in this area and in encouraging development of a Community Centre - sports hall - swimming pool on the site of the engineering works.

The SNP Councillor, **Janet Anderson**, is aware of the need for new housing but opposes the idea of building outside the town boundary, particularly in the Country Park area. The SNP as a party have campaigned for protecting the Scottish landscape and countryside.

Joyce Cunningham is the Social and Liberal Democrat Councillor. She is highly involved in environmental issues and used to be a member of Greenpeace and Friends of the Earth. She gained a great deal of publicity several years ago leading the campaign against the siting of a nuclear power station in the Region.

AREA OF PROPOSED NEW DEVELOPMENT

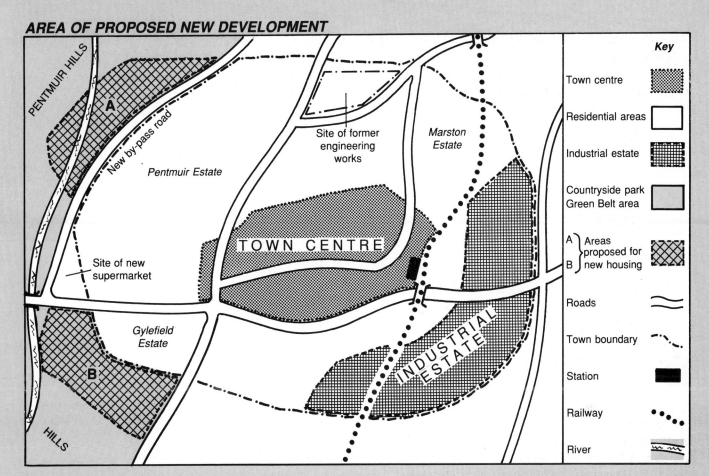

Key

Town centre

Residential areas

Industrial estate

Countryside park
Green Belt area

A ⎱ Areas
  ⎰ proposed for
B   new housing

Roads

Town boundary

Station

Railway

River

PENTMUIR HILLS

A

New by-pass road

Pentmuir Estate

Site of former
engineering
works

Marston
Estate

Site of new
supermarket

TOWN CENTRE

Gylefield
Estate

B

INDUSTRIAL
ESTATE

HILLS

The Marston area

Area proposed for housing development

What is a Country Park?

The Countryside (Scotland) Act 1967 defines a country park as: 'a park or pleasure ground in the countryside which by reason of its position in relation to major concentrations of population affords convenient opportunities to the public for enjoyment of the countryside or open-air recreation'.

In a simple language a country park is a place – usually quite close to a town or city – where anyone can enjoy the countryside and indulge in some outdoor activity. Perhaps you might want to learn something about wildlife and natural history – or just to relax in peaceful surroundings? Some country parks offer facilities for fishing, boating or sailing while others are situated in quiet woodlands or by the sea. There is something for everyone.

All country parks registered by the Countryside Commission for Scotland have a countryside ranger service to provide help and advice for visitors when needed. Many country parks also have visitor information centres and guided walks.

(Source: Countryside Commission for Scotland.)

The high cost of vandalism

"Last night John Simpson, his wife and two children returned home to 49 Muirton Road in the Marston area to find that vandals had broken into their house and wrecked the living-room.

"We are totally heart-broken." said Mr Simpson. This seems to happen around here all the time. There are so many empty houses waiting to be renovated or knocked down that no one seems to care or know what the future holds for this area. In some ways I can't blame the kids who do this for there is really nothing for them to do around here. There are no community centres or leisure centres. Just old houses and high unemployment. No one seems to care. The area has had the heart knocked out of it. It's time the Council started to help areas like this. . . . ."

(The Evening Courier)

Property guide

"Local house prices have been rising over the past year as local industry and commerce has grown and attracted new families into the area. A shortage in the supply of good quality housing has caused a dramatic increase in prices at this end of the market. The proposal to develop two new executive housing estates on the west side of town will help to ease this particular shortage and make the town more attractive to in-coming business people. . . . . . ."

(The Evening Courier)

A CTIVITIES

1. Act out the Council **debate** on the **issue** of whether planning permission should be given for the development of the two sites. There are three **motions** before the Council:

• That the Council approve planning permission for both sites.

• That the Council approve planning permission for one site only.

• That planning permission is refused for both sites.

Some pupils will have to take on the role of certain key Councillors in the debate: Sheila Thomson, John MacDonald, Alex Hamilton, James Millar, Andrew Weir, Janet Anderson and Joyce Cunningham. There will have to be a Convener or Chairperson of the Council, who will represent the Conservative Party since they are the majority. Other pupils in the class can take on the roles of the other Councillors from the four political parties represented on the Council. It is expected that the key Councillors mentioned above will play the major part in the debate but other Councillors would also be expected to speak.

The class will decide who will propose the various motions before the Council, and the speakers will need to prepare in advance of the debate what they are going to say. The background information, the map and the newspaper article will provide the basis of the information needed.

2. If it is possible the class should invite their local Councillor to explain to them the procedures used at a Council meeting.

3. After the debate the Council will have to take a vote to reach a decision. Remember there are three possible motions on which the Council can vote.

4. Discuss your Council result. Did all Councillors vote according to their party policy? If any Councillor voted against party policy, what were the issues which affected this vote? What combinations of parties were there in the votes for the various motions? What were the most important factors to emerge in the debate and did these affect the vote? Did anyone resign over this issue?

5. Design and write a newspaper article reporting the Council decision. Include quotes from the leading figures involved in this issue, giving their reaction to the decision and their future plans.

KEYWORDS

The following Keywords are used in this Unit. Make sure you have understood what they mean.

housing development	**campaign**
planning permission	**debate**
narrow majority	**motions**
safe majority	**issue**

PARTIES IN POLITICS

Why do we have political parties?

Hunting, Fishing or Farming -
The Divided Village

Once upon a time on a small island just off the mainland there lived a group of people. These islanders lived together in one village, near the coast and close to a river. The islanders lived by hunting, fishing and growing a few crops. The village had a sort of village council although the islanders would never have called it this. Nevertheless the adults would gather together in the evening in the largest hut in the village to talk about what had happened that day. The village council was usually a quiet affair with the younger people listening carefully to the wiser words of their elders. There were rarely arguments and the village usually worked closely together.

Now one year an unhappy time came to the village when for some reason the wild animals and fish became very scarce. The islanders had to live on wild plants, berries and the few crops that they grew. But they survived, and soon life got back to normal. The village council often talked about what had gone wrong. The older people warned that the gods had been angry and the disappearance of the wild animals and fish was a punishment. Some of the younger islanders became impatient with this and began to argue that the village should stop spending so much time on hunting and fishing and should concentrate more on growing crops. "But we have always lived by hunting and fishing – these are the ways of our people," cried the others. Soon the village council became full of argument and the council split into three groups. Some argued for the old ways of hunting and fishing, some argued for a mixture of hunting, fishing and farming, and

others argued for farming. Those who wanted the village to turn to farming began to form a close group and one evening one of the leaders of the farming group announced, "We are the largest group in the council now. We don't care for the ways of those who have gone before us. We think you older people are wrong. The village will now follow our way."

Division
In this story our island had been a united one because all the people in the village had agreed on how things would be done and how the islanders would live. In politics when people agree with each other on the main issues this is known as **consensus** of opinion. However, the village consensus began to fall apart when different points of view were expressed on how the islanders would live and how the village council would operate. In other words, **differences** or **divisions** appeared in the village and the islanders formed groups around these different beliefs.

It is in this way that **political parties** are formed. Political parties exist because there are differences or divisions within society. People with similar opinions group together because there is strength in numbers.

In our island story the villagers were divided over how the island could best provide food for itself and how the village council should be run. These are **economic** and **political** divisions. Sometimes people are divided by nationality, by religion, by wealth – rich and poor – or by their beliefs about how society should be organised. These divisions over beliefs are called **ideological** divisions. In the UK political parties are formed because people have different views about how our society should be governed. In some countries such as Communist countries it is argued that there are no divisions in society because all people are treated equally. Therefore there is no need for more than one political party – the Communist Party – which represents all the people.

QUESTIONS

1. Describe how the villagers on the island obtained their food.
2. Explain how the village council worked.
3. In what way could you say that there was a consensus about life on the island?
4. Explain in your own words how the village consensus came to be broken and how the islanders formed different groups. What were the issues around which different groups formed?
5. How does this story help us to understand why we have political parties in our democracies?
6. How do some Communist countries justify having only one political party – the Communist Party?

What do the political parties stand for?

CONSERVATIVES

"I'm a Conservative supporter. I'm a Conservative because I believe in freedom. I believe in freedom to choose the way I want to live without people or Government interfering. This is what we Conservatives call **'freedom of choice'**. People should be free to choose the house they want to live in, the school they want to send their children to and the doctor or hospital they want to go to. And if people want to buy these services privately then they should be allowed to. I believe in private companies making and selling their goods and services without interference. I believe in competition and profit. It is only through competition that the best individuals and the best companies can come to the top and allow Britain to compete. People should be encouraged to look after themselves more. Of course there are the poor, the old and the sick and the Government must care for these through the **Welfare State**.

Labour

"I'm a Labour supporter. I'm a Labour supporter because I believe in **equality**. I believe that everyone, whether rich or poor, man or woman, black or white, should have an equal opportunity to do well in life. This is impossible if the wealthy are allowed to buy the best services for themselves – the best education and the best medical services. The State should provide the best schools and the **National Health Service** the best doctors and hospitals. Then there would be no need to buy services privately. I believe also that those who are well-off have a duty to help those who are less well-off. Those with most money should pay most in taxes to pay for the services of those most in need, such as the old and the unemployed.

I believe in private companies providing goods and services. But I also believe that some things that provide for the nation, like electricity, gas, transport, are too important to be run for profit only.

These industries also provide a service for the public and should be run by the State as **nationalised industries**. I believe in a strong Britain with strong armed forces but I do not believe in nuclear weapons. These are a waste of money. They do not help to make Britain safe. They only help to make it a target."

But we cannot afford to allow everyone to depend on the State. The unemployed will never find work if they are not encouraged to go out and look for work. I also believe in a strong Britain which can protect itself through strong armed forces and through nuclear weapons."

"I'm a Social and Liberal Democratic supporter. I used to be a Liberal but now I call myself a Democrat since my old party joined forces with the Social Democratic Party. I'm a Democrat because I'm a moderate who believes in the middle way. This country has suffered because it has, over the years, swung from one extreme to another – from Conservative, to Labour and back to Conservative again. The Labour Party does what the Trades Unions tell it and the Conservatives do what big business tells it. We do not need to go to extremes. We can have private services but we should also have good and efficient State services. We can encourage people to do well without neglecting those who do not succeed. The voters do not want the extremes of the Conservatives or of Labour. They do not vote for this but this is what they get because of our voting system. I believe in changing the voting system to bring in a moderate Government which the majority of the people have voted for. I believe in a strong Britain with strong armed forces. I do not want Britain to defend itself with nuclear weapons but I do not want to get rid of them until all sides agree to scrap them."

What it would be like in an independent Scotland

The promise of independence lies inside the next UK ball[o] boxes to be counted, says the SNP. And if the UK does break up, the party will not be found wanting in organisation. A draft written constitution has long existed. A constitutional convention to add further refinements ma[y] soon get under way.

The Queen would remain as head of State. A Prime Minister would be appointed by a single-tier Parliament sitting on Calton Hill in Edinburgh, the 200 members having been elected by a hybrid system of constituency an[d] proportional representation.

Negotiations would be opened with the Treasury in London for the transfer of Scotland's share of revenues, n[ot] just the oil money. A Scottish army, navy and air force would come into being. Membership of NATO would be renegotiated as would the terms of membership of the EE[C.] Foreign affairs and defence policy would be controlled from inside Scotland's borders.

Customs posts at the border, if they were ever likely a[t] all, will have been rendered irrelevant by the single European market.

The SNP wants Scotland to take its place within the European family of nations, no longer attached to the sou[th] of Britain by political bonds, only by geographical ones.

(source: *Scotland on Sunday*, 13 November 198[8])

SCOTTISH NATIONAL PARTY

Play the Scottish card

The principal aim of the Scottish National Party is to win support for the establishment of an independent Scottish Parliament. This Parliament would allow the Scottish people to win their national freedom, and provide the power to change our country for the better.

One in every three Scots now wants Independence and only votes for the SNP count in the battle to win full independence for our nation.

Scotland in Europe

Scotland has stood on the sidelines for too long. The SNP say that it is time to demand our rightful place in the EEC as an independent European nation. Scots can and must play our part in creating a better Europe where Jobs, Security and Peace are available for all citizens. This is a policy for Scotland as an outward looking European nation. In contrast the other parties want to keep Scotland isolated and unrepresented as a mere region of England.

(source: Scottish National Party)

Extracts from Scottish National Party literature

A CTIVITIES

1. Read the extracts about the Scottish National Party and write a short statement beginning, "I'm a Scottish National Party supporter...."

2. Find out about the Green Party. What are its aims?

3. Write out the following list of party policies and beside each one write which party (parties) you think would support the statement:

a) keeping taxes low;

b) bringing about independence for Scotland;

c) changing our system of voting in elections;

d) encouraging private medicine and private schools;

e) working with the trades unions;

f) getting rid of nuclear weapons only when all sides agree to scrap them;

g) building up the Welfare State;

h) placing most industries under private control;

i) making those who can afford it pay for medical services within the National Health Service;

j) spending money on public projects to create jobs;

k) getting rid of nuclear power stations and keeping the environment clean.

4. At election time all the political parties publish a document listing all their policies. This is called a **manifesto**. Choose a political party with which you think you agree and write an election manifesto explaining what your policies are and encouraging your classmates to vote for you.

5. Split into groups of four. Each member of the group should choose one of the four main political parties in Scotland, i.e. Labour, SNP, Conservative and SLD. Have a group discussion on which party is best for the future of Scotland.

KEYWORDS

The following Keywords are used in this Unit. Make sure you have understood what they mean.

consensus	freedom of choice
differences	Welfare State
divisions	equality
political party	National Health Service
economic divisions	nationalised industries
political divisions	manifesto
ideological	

POLICY BECOMES LAW

Locked up for breaking locks

A man was jailed today after admitting to three charges of breaking and entering. Sentencing Angus Mactavish of 101, Craigford Drive to two years imprisonment. . . . . .

(source: *Craigford Courier*, 30 January 1989.)

When we read stories like this we call them crime stories. A crime has been committed, a **law** has been broken. We have laws to protect us against the actions of others. Schools have rules which are similar to laws.

School rules – the law of the land

In Unit 1, at Craigford School the situation wasn't as clear cut as the crime reported in the story above. The students of Craigford were able to **participate** in making a decision which affected the running of the school. The decision was made after the students' representatives were able to make a suggestion at a meeting with the Headteacher. The new rule would help the school to run more smoothly. Many other aspects of school life are organised to help the running of the school. The school timetable, the subjects you are able to choose, and the length of the school day; are all examples of this kind.

Most of the laws with which Parliament deals are like this. They are passed to organise the way things are done in our society. Political parties offer us a choice of policies and when we elect a Government we give them the right to put these policies into practice.

In this unit we are going to look at changes in the law. By the end of the unit you will know how a new law is made. You will be able to investigate for yourself how a new idea becomes a law and you will also find out why most people obey the laws of the land.

QUESTIONS

1. In your notebook make up four lists under the following headings:
   a) School rules (e.g. no eating in class);
   b) School organisation (e.g. the school must have a timetable);
   c) Laws (e.g. you must not break into a bank);
   d) Government policies (e.g. people should be encouraged to buy their own houses).

2. Use the words in the box to complete the following sentences in your notebooks.

rules	eating	bullying
school timetable	affect	school

Every week at Craigford High School students do things that are against school . . . . . . Some of these are small things like . . . . in class, others are more important like . . . . The school tries to stop these things because they . . . . others.
Every year the . . . . has to have a . . . . so that students and teachers will know which classes are on during each day.

3. Try to write a similar paragraph dealing with the laws which govern our lives.

Ideas into law

When a new law is made there is a great deal of activity which goes on behind the scenes before we hear about it.

1. Somebody will come up with an idea for a new law. It may be political party or a pressure group.

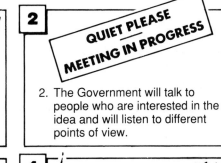

2. The Government will talk to people who are interested in the idea and will listen to different points of view.

3. The Government will publish its ideas in various ways.

4. The new idea will be made into a law by Parliament.

5. The new law will be put into practice by the Government. It may be enforced by the police and the courts.

Read the following summary of how the **Youth Training Scheme** (YTS) was brought into being.

The Youth Training Scheme began in 1983 and was a new way of organising training for young people in Britain.

- It was planned from 1981 because the Youth Opportunities Programme (YOP) was not successful in providing the quality of training that Britain needed. There were many criticisms of that scheme from young people, trades unions and politicians.

- In May 1981 the Training Commission (then the Manpower services Commission) published a document, *A Training Initiative*, and received a large number of responses from interested organisations.

- In December 1981 the Government published a White Paper followed by a Planning Document. The job of planning was given to a group made up of representatives of industry, the Confederation of British Industry (CBI), trades unions, The Trades Union Congress (TUC), local authorities and education.

- During 1982 the new scheme went through all the **consultative stages** (see diagram above), during which time the Government had to accept advice from the CBI and the TUC to increase the pay for trainees. At the same time the Government insisted that young people who refused a place on a scheme would lose six weeks of benefit (income support). (income support).

- In September 1983 the new Youth Training Scheme was introduced. The scheme guaranteed one year's training for any school leaver who did not have a job.

A CTIVITY

Make up a chart showing the different stages that this idea had to go through before becoming a new law.

Since this law was put into practice many points of view have been expressed about it. The scheme has been changed in various ways and now the Government says that any young school leaver can be guaranteed two full years on YTS. The Government has also made a rule that if a young person refuses to take a place then they will lose the right to *any* benefit. It means that a young person aged sixteen must now choose from amongst the following:
a) Staying on at school; b) Joining a YTS;
c) Going to College;   d) Finding a job;
e) Being unemployed without benefit until the age of eighteen.

The two-year youth training scheme

... YTS had become an obvious way of screening young people for recruitment. Over half the managing agents and nearly three-quarters of the other work experience providers have said they use the scheme in this way. In return for providing rudimentary training, employers are able to pick and choose their recruits from a pool of cheap trainees. . .

The latest follow-up survey shows that the young people who left YTS between April 1986 and September 1987, 59% were in work, 22% were unemployed, and 16% were in education or other training (11% of these had joined another YTS scheme). Those trainees who were most likely to become unemployed were living in inner cities or the depressed regions. They were likely to have fewer qualifications, and to come from ethnic minority backgrounds.

(source: *Social Studies Review*, Vol. 4, No. 1.)

"I've not been able to find a place in three months because they say the scheme is over-subscribed," [a young school leaver] said earlier this week.

Inquiries by The Scotsman have confirmed that there are more than 20,000 16 and 17 year-olds throughout Scotland chasing places on the YTS, on which there are fewer than 9,000 places available.

(source: *The Scotsman*, 3 November 1988.)

Employers' reasons for taking part in YTS

	% of establishments
Advantages to the employer	
Screening for good employees	42
Savings on labour costs	32
Help with training budget	9
Personal or business obligation	7
Good for employer's image	6
Other advantages	18
Social Reasons	
Wanted to do something to help young people	45
Seriousness of youth employment problem	22
Obligation to society to help deal with serious social problem	15
Obligation to the industry to play part in training	10
Other social reasons	7
Number of employers surveyed	1,000

(source: *Employment Gazette*, June 1986.)
Note: Percentages add up to more than 100% as respondents could give more than one answer.

A CTIVITIES

1. Using the information given, list the evidence which suggests that the YTS scheme has not succeeded in the way in which it was intended.

2. Some of the changes to the YTS scheme are fairly recent. What changes would you like to see in the way the YTS scheme works?

3. Discuss the reasons why employers use the YTS in their organisations. You could carry out a local survey.

Today in Parliament

Every year during the autumn the Government sets out the new laws it is going to make during the following parliamentary **session**. These are announced briefly by the Queen to Members of Parliament in the Queen's Speech at the opening of Parliament in October. They will become laws during the following year. Most of the new laws will be Government policies. This means that they will be ideas which the Government described in its party manifesto before the previous election, and pledged itself to carry out if it was elected. Where do these ideas come from? (Look again at page 61.)

During the passage of a Bill through parliament there are opportunities to alter the new law slightly but on almost every occasion the Government is able to pass the laws it wants to. This is because the Government has a majority in Parliament and most Members of Parliament will support their own party. Pressure Groups will try to make changes which they see as important.

Here is a more detailed diagram which shows what actually happens in Parliament.

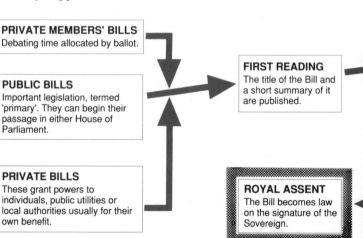

PRIVATE MEMBERS' BILLS
Debating time allocated by ballot.

PUBLIC BILLS
Important legislation, termed 'primary'. They can begin their passage in either House of Parliament.

PRIVATE BILLS
These grant powers to individuals, public utilities or local authorities usually for their own benefit.

FIRST READING
The title of the Bill and a short summary of it are published.

ROYAL ASSENT
The Bill becomes law on the signature of the Sovereign.

Making it work

Once a policy has become a law then it has to be put into effect. In the case of some laws it is up to the police and the law courts to enforce the law. In most cases, though, the new law simply affects the way some part of our lives is organised.

Every year the Chancellor of the Exchequer publishes a **budget**. This sets out how the Government will collect money from us in **taxes** in the following year. Every year a new law called the Finance Act gives the Government the power to do this. The law is put into effect by the Inland Revenue which collects the taxes and thousands of employers who deduct the taxes due from every worker's pay packet.

If there is a new law about schools, then it will be the Scottish Education Department and the Regional Councils who have to deal with it.

If the new law is about housing then it will be District Councils and Scottish Homes, an agency set up by the Government to carry out their housing policies, who deal with it.

Even so, if there is some dispute about how a law is being put into effect the courts may still become involved.

The law of the land?

Parliament does its best to pass laws which will be supported by people in the country as a whole. The Government has a majority in Parliament and is elected to govern the country. As we have seen, Parliament represents all of us so when a law is passed we are all expected to observe it.

The parties in opposition to the Government criticise their policies and argue against the Bills as they are going through Parliament.

If a different political party wins the next election then the new Government may decide to change things that the previous Government has done. In the meantime though, what about people who do not accept a particular law? For example:

There are laws which allow experiments to be carried out on live animals.

HOW BILLS GO THROUGH PARLIAMENT

SECOND READING
The broad principles are debated and voted upon. The Lords do not vote on Bills at this stage.

COMMITTEE STAGE
The Bill is debated line by line and attempts are made to amend, wreck or redraft the measure by MPs and peers. In the Commons, MPs debate selected amendments in a standing committee away from the Chamber. The Lords hold this debate on the floor of the House.

REPORT STAGE
Changes are made in response to points made or trailed in committee.

THIRD READING
The Bill in its final form is debated and voted upon. The Lords are allowed further scope to amend the Bill at this stage.

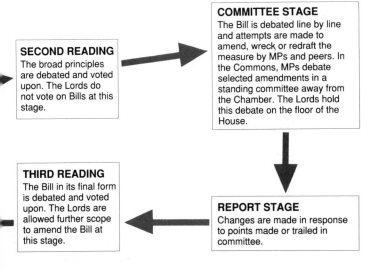

Academics deny breaking law on animal experiments

By ROB EDWARDS

GLASGOW University's Faculty of Veterinary Medicine has encountered serious problems in fulfilling new legislation on animal experiments, according to confidential documents leaked to an animal rights group.

Animal Concern (Scotland) ...claims that the documents show that the university was in a "terrible muddle" over how to implement a 1986 Act designed to tighten up the rules governing vivisection.

(source: *The Scotsman*, 14 November 1988.)

In Scotland there were groups who encouraged people not to pay the Poll Tax/Community Charge.

People who cheat the Government may be treated in very different ways.

It is sometimes thought that drunken driving isn't taken seriously enough.

Councillor Not To Pay Tax

..."I have never knowingly broken any law before," adds Councillor Johnston, "but this Tory poll tax is different."

(source: *Livingston Post*, 20 October 1988.)

Prominent poll tax rebels to be named

By PETER JONES

THE NAMES of prominent people who will declare their intention not to pay the poll tax or community charge, are to be announced. . . as part of the much stronger political fight against the Government that voters in Govan had demonstrated they wanted.

(source: *The Scotsman*, 14 November 1988.)

THE CASUALTY LIST

The bitterness of families of innocent victims killed by drunk drivers whose punishment, they believe, too often does not fit the crime, provided the spur for the Campaign Against Drinking and Driving. Since its information three years ago, CADD has attracted more than 800 members, all of whom have suffered the loss of a loved one through drunk driving. . . The Government is considering changes in the road traffic law that may go some way towards justice for the drunk driver who kills but is not punished adequately.

- Twenty per cent of the road deaths in Britain–more than 1,000 every year–are linked to drink.
- Ten per cent of all reported accidents involving injuries are due to drinking and driving–amounting to 24,000 accidents.
- Twenty seven per cent of drivers and 22 per cent of motorcycle riders killed have blood alcohol concentrations over the legal limit.
- Seventy seven per cent of the British public are in favour of the introduction of random breath tests, according to a NOP survey in 1987.

(source: *The Observer*, 13 November 1988.)

SCANDAL OF THE REAL SCROUNGERS

In the eyes of the law, all people may be equal but from the Government there is a shaming discrepancy in the differing treatment of tax and social security offenders.

Cost of dole fraud £500 million
Cost of tax fraud £5,500 million
Number of prosecutions 14,000 (dole fraud)
Number of prosecutions 20 (tax fraud)

(source: *The Observer*, 23 October 1988.)

A recent survey asked people to comment on the following statement, "The law should always be obeyed even if a particular law is wrong". The result showed:

Agree	45%
Neither agree/nor disagree	24%
Disagree	31%

Q UESTIONS

1. Where do most of the ideas for new laws come from?
2. Why is the Government almost always able to pass the laws it wants to?
3. Who might be able to influence a law as it is passing through Parliament?
4. List four organisations who are responsible for putting laws into effect.

A CTIVITIES

1. a) Carry out a local survey of people's comments on the above statement about obeying the law, or (b) investigate attitudes towards obeying a particular law.
2. Compare your results with the above table, if you choose (a).
3. You could try to ask different age groups the same questions, or ask people which political party they support. See if you get different results from different groups.

Televising Parliament

People who want to know what is going on in Parliament can find out in several ways. They can sit in the Public Gallery, read *Hansard*, listen to *Today in Parliament* on the radio, read the Parliamentary reports in some daily newspapers or watch TV.

Turn on the Commons TV cameras

SUNDAY EXPRESS EXCLUSIVE POLL

Asked whether they were in favour of television in Parliament [people polled by Telephone Surveys] replied:

Yes . . . . 65 per cent.

No . . . . 35 per cent.

Most of those in favour–a hefty 41 per cent–said they wanted debates on TV to find out what happens when great national issues were discussed.

Others favoured TV coverage because it would bring national affairs to life (11 per cent), provide good entertainment (10 per cent), give people the chance to see decisions made (16 per cent) and identify those guilty of bad behaviour (8 per cent).

Those against were mainly opposed because they thought coverage would be uninteresting and boring while a third of the opponents said MPs would be tempted to play to the cameras.

A small percentage of people against television–eight per cent–thought it would bring Parliament into disrepute, while one in ten of the critics was worried about the break in tradition.

Most people also believe there would be little impact on behaviour among the young if the Commons is televised.

When asked if it would encourage bad behaviour among young people they replied:

Yes . . . . 28 per cent

No . . . . 63 per cent

Don't know . . . . 9 per cent

...When asked if minority pressure groups would be tempted to stage demos, the replies were:

Yes . . . . 72 per cent

No . . . . 20 per cent

Don't know . . . . 8 per cent

(source: *Sunday Express Newspaper*, 7 February 1988.)

A CTIVITIES

1. Carry out a survey in your area using questions similar to those suggested in the article. (This was written nine months before the House of Commons was televised.)

2. Collect newspaper cuttings about the behaviour of Members of Parliament in the House of Commons.

3. Choose one of the arguments in favour of televising Parliament or one of the arguments against. Students who are studying the same argument should work together and write down ideas which they think would support their argument. Try to find information to back up your argument.

4. Report your group's findings to the class. Listen carefully to groups who have researched different points of view. You may find that your own research helps you to make your point of view count in the discussion which follows.

5. Write a report on your own point of view after the discussion.

Q UESTIONS

1. Why are a majority of people in favour of the televising of Parliament?

2. Why did some people oppose the televising of Parliament?

KEYWORDS

The following Keywords are used in this Unit. Make sure you have understood what they mean.

law   **benefit**   **budget**

participate   **session**   **taxes**

consultative stages Youth Training Scheme (YTS)

4

PRESSURE

INFLUENCING DECISIONS

In Chapter 2 we saw how a trade union and its members tried to persuade the Government to help with the problem of saving jobs at their factory.

In that example the trade union was trying to help a particular group of people. Its members were trying to influence, or put pressure on, the factory owners and the Government. To help them do this the workers of Caterpillar used many methods, including meetings of members, public meetings, giving out leaflets, selling badges, collecting names on a petition, walking on marches, meeting with Members of Parliament and attracting attention from the mass media. MPs asked questions in the House of Commons, workers went to Westminster to speak to Government Ministers, people wrote to their own MPs, to Government Ministers and to the Prime Minister.

These are some of the ways in which **pressure groups** work, and in using them the people were able to take part in what they saw as an important fight for jobs in their community. In situations like this people get much more involved in politics than is often the case. It is not always enough to **participate** simply by voting at elections. Sometimes more immediate action needs to be taken.

Pressure groups offer different ways of influencing the decisions that affect our lives. This may involve talking about concerns with friends, giving money to a campaign or charity, or joining an organisation like Greenpeace, and becoming a worker in the campaign.

You may have read about the work of Greenpeace in newspapers or seen its activities on TV. Greenpeace puts pressure on governments around the world to try to persuade them to stop damaging our environment. Greenpeace claims considerable success in this work. Through its educational material and by taking **direct action**, it has influenced public opinion, and made people more aware of the importance of **environmental issues**.

GREENPEACE STANDS FOR A SAFE AND NUCLEAR-FREE WORLD FRESH AIR CLEAN WATER THE PROTECTION OF WILDLIFE AND THEIR HABITATS

Greenpeace has: Stopped the French testing nuclear weapons in the atmosphere. Helped bring an end to commercial whaling. Prevented baby seals being killed in Newfoundland and the Orkney Isles. Won an agreement in principle to end radioactive waste discharges into the Irish Sea. Won agreements to end the dumping of chemical sludges into the North Sea.

Forced an end to the burning of hazardous wastes in the North Sea. Helped block proposals to dispose of radioactive wastes at a number of sites within the UK....

Won a review of import procedures of endangered species products into the EEC. Helped persuade the Government to spend £200m cleaning Britain's beaches and £600m cleaning aerial discharges from coal-fired power stations.

Greenpeace is an international environmental pressure group which maintains complete independence from all political parties anywhere in the world.

GREENPEACE CAMPAIGNS

Greenpeace campaigns to save the whales • to stop nuclear weapons tests • to protect seals, dolphins, porpoises and sea turtles • to stop the disposal of radioactive waste and dangerous chemicals at sea • to close down nuclear power stations and nuclear reprocessing plants • to stop acid rain and protect the atmosphere • to reduce the trade in endangered species products.

*Q*UESTIONS

1. What are the main concerns of Greenpeace?

2. What is the connection between all of these concerns?

3. What is the difference between Greenpeace and a political party?

4. Choose one of the Greenpeace actions. Explain how your life might have been affected by it.

Pressure groups

You have learned that the Government passes laws which affect many aspects of our lives and that, closer to home, the Local Council is responsible for providing services which many of us use. In almost every case there are pressure groups which try to influence these decisions.

In Chapter 3 Unit 4 you saw how some pressure groups play an important part, working alongside the Government when new laws are passed.

Here are examples of how some pressure groups have worked together to influence changes in the law.

Jimmy's dad wouldn't let him go to football matches before **alcohol was banned from football grounds**.

Groups involved - Scottish Football Association (SFA)
- The Police Federation
- Scottish Professional Footballers Association

Mrs McDade had her **Housing Benefit cut** when new rules were brought in during April 1988. She needs help from groups such as:
- Local Welfare Rights Group
- Convention of Scottish Local Authorities (COSLA)
- Shelter – a housing campaign group
- Age Concern

Jack Braid was **unemployed** and had dealings with the Department of Social Security and the Enterprise Initiative. He needs help from groups such as:
- Local Training Agency
- Local Trades Council
- Trades Union Congress (TUC)
- Confederation of British Industry (CBI)

Joanna Giles was concerned about the **contamination of food with Salmonella** and especially with the **treatment of animals in food production**. These issues are the concerns of groups such as:
- National Farmers Union (NFU)
- Nutrition Foundation
- Friends of the Earth
- The Animals Rights Group

*A*CTIVITIES

As a class you can get a much clearer idea of the kinds of activities that pressure groups are involved in if you set out to investigate the work of a range of pressure groups. This process may take some time so you will have to plan with your teacher how to organise your work. To get started quickly it may be best to begin with some local groups.

1. Make up a list of local groups for your class to use. The following organisations may be able to help you.

Regional Council   District Council
Social Work Department
Voluntary Organisations Council
Citizens Advice Bureau   Local newspaper
School and local library
Community Education Department.
You could set up a **database** on local groups on your school computers.

2. Make up a list of other pressure groups and their work. Your teacher will help you with this. You will find that the national newspapers are a good source of names and you may find addresses in telephone directories or in your school or local library. Remember that trades unions and employers organisations are also important interest groups, so you could start by contacting industrial or commercial firms in your area. (See next page for suggestions on planning your approach.)

THE SPASTICS SOCIETY
FOR PEOPLE WITH CEREBRAL PALSY

THE INDUSTRIAL DISEASES SUFFERERS' GROUP

NCCL
National Council for Civil Liberties
We are committed to the defence and extension of civil liberties in the United Kingdom and to the rights and freedom recognised by international law.

Reward offered to vivisection 'moles'

WORKERS in Scottish laboratories conducting experiments on animals are being offered money to break the law.

Animal Concern (Scotland) is offering a £100 reward to researchers and other employers prepared to risk a jail sentence by "blowing the whistle" on the work being carried out in their laboratories.

(source: *The Scotsman*, 14 April 1988.)

Boycott the products of apartheid!

For years the people of South Africa and Namibia have called for the world to shun Apartheid and pressurise the white minority to bring the system to an end. Today it is more important than ever to BOYCOTT APARTHEID goods in our shops.
(Scottish Committee, Anti Apartheid Movement.)

PLAN YOUR APPROACH.

a) ON THE PHONE

i)   Make up a sheet like the one shown here.

ON THE PHONE

Name Lowland Regional Council – Social Work

Phone Number 42320

"Hello my name is Julie Black I would like to speak to somebody who could help me with a project I am doing at Craigford High School."

"I am trying to make up a list of local groups which have dealings with the Social Work Department."

(At this stage you do have to be clear about the kind of information you want.)

"Thank you very much Mr Russell I look forward to hearing from you."

---

ii)   You may wish to write a letter following your phone call.

b) WRITING A LETTER

i)   Write a rough copy of your letter like the one shown here.

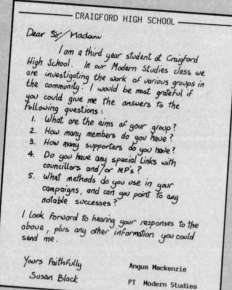

— CRAIGFORD HIGH SCHOOL —

Dear Sir/Madam

I am a third year student at Craigford High School. In our Modern Studies class we are investigating the work of various groups in the community. I would be most grateful if you could give me the answers to the following questions:

1. What are the aims of your group?
2. How many members do you have?
3. How many supporters do you have?
4. Do you have any special links with councillors and/or MP's?
5. What methods do you use in your campaigns, and can you point to any notable successes?

I look forward to hearing your responses to the above, plus any other information you could send me.

Yours faithfully

Susan Black

Angus Mackenzie

PT Modern Studies

ii)   Your teacher should check your letter and sign it beside your own signature.

iii)   In most cases you should enclose a stamped addressed envelope with your letter, especially if you are contacting a group which doesn't have much money because it is a **charity** or is run mainly by voluntary workers.

c) SENDING A QUESTIONNAIRE

i)   Your questions should be straightforward and ask for simple answers. See the example shown here.

A SIMPLE QUESTIONNAIRE

Thank you very much for taking the trouble to complete this questionnaire.

NAME OF GROUP –

CRAIGFORD WELFARE RIGHTS GROUP

1. How many members do you have?   ....

2. How many supporters do you have? (e.g. as indicated by public opinion)   ....

3. How many workers do you have? paid   ....
   unpaid   ....

4. What methods do you use to influence decision-makers?

   ✓ / ✗

   meet councillors   ....
   meet council officials   ....
   inform the press   ....
   campaign in public   ....
   organise protests   ....
   other – please comment   ....

5. Can you point to any particular success? Please give details.

---

ii)   The class should agree about the main questions so that you can compare different groups.

iii)   You might want to add some questions of your own, but not too many.

3.   As you gather information on each group make up a file about its work. Gather information about your group from other sources as well, e.g. you might interview one of the group's workers, or one of the group's clients, and you could collect cuttings from local or national newspapers.

4.   Write a report about the work of your chosen group. You should include material to show how it works and how successful it is.

5.   You might choose to make a brief taped report about your group.

6.   Your class could make a classroom or school display about groups in your area, or about the work of national pressure groups, such as Scottish Women's Aid or Shelter (Scotland).

While we can all join pressure groups if we wish, it would appear that some people are able to exert much more influence than others. This is done through what is known as Parliamentary **lobbying**.

Party goes on for the lobbyists

...Lobbyists – or public affairs consultants as they like to be termed – all have the same objective: to give their clients access to key opinion formers. Contrary to popular mythology, most lobbyists are not sleazy sharks with dirty raincoats. They are more likely to be mild mannered ex-civil servants, parliamentary research assistants, or former MPs...

While their methods may differ, many would admit that sometimes their tactics are more below-the-belt than below-the-line.

'... I remember a group who staged a whisky-tasting party for MPs to coincide with a very dull environment Bill in which they had no interest. When the party ended, the Members were steered into the nearby House [of Commons]...'

Backbenchers are however more likely to be swayed with relevant case-history material than hospitality... The real issue facing the industry now is the proposed introduction of a US-style register of lobbyists...

But the snag is, who would be included on the register and who wouldn't? The suggestion that people might have to sit lobbying exams to qualify is clearly very silly, for how can someone be tested on a system which is largely based on unwritten rules and gentlemen's agreements? All the same, a register might break the conspiracy of silence, which surrounds the lobbying industry.

(**Anita Chaudhuri**)

(source: *The Observer*, 15 November 1987.)

Q UESTIONS

1. What kind of people work as lobbyists? Give examples from the article.

2. What methods do pressure groups or lobbyists use to influence Members of Parliament?

3. How can lobbying be controlled?

4. Is lobbying fair or does it give some people too much influence?

KEYWORDS

The following Keywords are used in this Unit. Make sure you have understood what they mean.

pressure groups environmental issues
participate database charity
direct action lobbying

SURVEYS ON ACTIONS

In Chapter 2, Unit 4, we ended by asking whether people really believed that the political system was able to represent their views properly. In this Unit you have seen that there are in fact many other ways for people to make their views known and to have some real influence on decisions that affect their lives.

Here are some more ideas about how people really behave in relation to political issues.

How to protest

% Saying that different forms of protest should 'definitely' or 'probably' be allowed

	%
Organising public meetings to protest against the government	83
Publishing pamphlets to protest against the government	78
Organising protest marches and demonstrations	58
Organising a nationwide strike of all workers against the government	28
Occupying a government office and stopping work there for several days	10
Seriously damaging government buildings	2

(source: *British Social Attitudes*. The 1987 Report.)

Would you protest?

	Would do	Had ever done	Believed 'very' or 'quite' effective
	%	%	%
Sign petition	65	34	45
Contact your MP	52	11	50
Contact radio, TV or newspaper	15	3	58
Speak to influential person	15	3	38
Contact government department	12	3	26
Go on protest or demonstration	11	6	21
Raise issue in organisation you already belong to	10	5	32
Form group of like-minded people	8	2	26

(source: *British Social Attitudes*. The 1987 Report.)

TAKING ACTION

It would seem that while we don't have much confidence in the politicians themselves, we do believe that we can and should be able to do things for ourselves which politicians will have to listen to.

A CTIVITIES

1. Carry out the same surveys in your area.

2. Compare the results with the national figures.

3. Collect pamphlets and newspaper cuttings about some of these ways of influencing decisions.

4. In your group, discuss this issue. Why do you think so few people have actually done anything mentioned in the surveys?

12

HOW PRESSURE GROUPS WORK

In this Unit we will look at the work of a real **pressure group**. This is an organisation which brings together people who share common ideas or aims and wish to try to persuade others – either the public or people in authority – that these ideas or aims should be put into practice.

The pressure group we look at is the National Viewers' and Listeners' Association which aims to improve the quality of radio and television programmes. Its President is Mrs Mary Whitehouse.

PRESIDENT: MRS MARY WHITEHOUSE, C.B.E.

NATIONAL VIEWERS' AND LISTENERS' ASSOCIATION

Ever thought you wanted to switch off?

PRESIDENT: MRS. MARY WHITEHOUSE, C.B.E. ARDLEIGH, COLCHESTER, ESSEX, CO7 7RH Tel: Colchester (0206) 230123

National VALA Believes

- THAT CHRISTIAN VALUES ARE BASIC TO THE HEALTH AND WELLBEING OF OUR NATION AND THEREFORE CALLS ON THE BROADCASTING AUTHORITIES TO REVERSE THE CURRENT HUMANIST APPROACH TO SOCIAL, RELIGIOUS AND PERSONAL ISSUES.

- That the Broadcasting Authorities should fulfil their legal obligations to ensure "that nothing is included in the programmes which offends against good taste or decency or is likely to encourage or incite to crime or lead to disorder or to be offensive to public feeling" and "that the programmes maintain a proper balance . . ." (Television Act 1954). (Broadcasting Act 1981).

- That violence on television contributes significantly to the increase of violence in society and should be curtailed.

- That the use of swearing and blasphemy are destructive of our culture and our faith and that the Broadcasting Authorities are remiss in allowing it.

- That sexual innuendo and explicit sex trivialise and cheapen human relationships and undermine marriage and family life.

- That the media is indivisible and that the quality of film, theatre and publishing inevitably affects broadcasting standards.

National VALA Aims

1. To encourage viewers and listeners to react effectively to programme content.

2. To stimulate public and parliamentary discussion on the effects of broadcasting on the individual, the family and society.

3. To secure effective legislation to control obscenity and pornography in the media – including broadcasting.

ACTION – THINGS YOU CAN DO

▷ REMEMBER – YOUR EFFORT COUNTS.
NO ONE ELSE CAN PLAY YOUR PART. ◁

1 NEW MEMBERS
A large and active membership is essential if National VALA's aims are to be achieved. COULD YOU ORGANISE A MEETING LOCALLY TO PROMOTE THE WORK AND ENROL NEW MEMBERS? COULD YOU CONDUCT A LOCAL SCHEME TO RECRUIT NEW MEMBERS BY LETTER?

2 VIEWING, LISTENING, WRITING
Broadcasters need to be made aware of public response to their programmes. Letters should be sent IN APPRECIATION of the good as well as criticism of the bad.

3 ACTION GROUP/BRANCHES
Local Action Groups and Branches are most important because many people, although concerned, will often take action only with the support of others in a group.
WILL YOU HELP TO FORM A BRANCH OR ACTION GROUP?

4 DEAR MEMBER OF PARLIAMENT
Parliament is ultimately responsible for Broadcasting. MPs rarely have time to watch or listen so keep them informed of what is being transmitted and your reaction to it.

5 YOU SAW WHAT (!) ON TELEVISION?
Monitoring is a vital part of National VALA's work and HQ. MUST BE CONSTANTLY FED WITH INFORMATION ON PROGRAMMES. Details are crucial: programme, date, time, channel. . . violence; swearing and blasphemy; the exploitation of sex.

Q UESTIONS

1. What are the aims of the National Viewers' and Listeners' Association (VALA)?

2. What does National VALA believe in?

3. What actions can people take to help to improve the quality of radio and television programmes?

25 YEARS ON!

1989 SILVER JUBILEE YEAR

It will be 25 years on January 28th 1989 since the late Rev Basil Buckland and his wife Norah, of Longton, Stoke on Trent, and Ernest and Mary Whitehouse launched the Clean Up TV Campaign which later became the National Viewers' and Listeners' Association.

Nearly 6 million signatures on various petitions, new legislation to protect children (1987), to control indecent displays (1981) and 'video nasties' (1984), not to mention many overseas tours, 5 published books and countless radio and television programmes later, we will celebrate our Silver Jubilee on Saturday March 11th 1989 in the presence of the Chairman of the Broadcasting Standards Council as our Guest Speaker.

REMEMBER – WE COUNT ON YOUR SUPPORT THE MORE MEMBERS NATIONAL VALA HAS-THE GREATER ITS IMPACT.

SPECIAL LETTER CAMPAIGN

Your MPs name

The House of Commons
London
SW1A 0AA

your local library or Citizens Advice Bureau can tell you the name of your MP if you are not sure

Dear M

URGENT

Please write to your MP asking for immediate Government action on Pornography and Media Obscenity

---

FULL MARKS FOR – EastEnders

Let's give credit where credit is due and propose a vote of thanks to Julia Smith, the producer of EastEnders, and others involved – one suspects at a very high level in the BBC – for the undoubted improvement of that programme....

Our great concern has been that this series with its story lines involving rape, arson (petrol bomb attack) – even possibly the burning alive of one of the characters – prostitution, obscene gestures, threats with knives, calls for castration, foul language, has totally violated the concept of family viewing time and it is a matter of the utmost importance that such a concept is not destroyed...

Although the "cleaning up" of EastEnders took some time to work through it certainly does appear, at the time of writing, to be working. But we cannot take anything for granted!

SEVEN DAYS VIOLENCE No 3
Alarming report shows
1 in 4 programmes violent

A monitoring project to assess the level of violence in television programmes was carried out by National VALA between 12 and 19 days after the shooting tragedy at Hungerford. Immediately after the shooting ITV pulled out their schedules a particularly violent episode of 'The Professionals', 'Nevada Smith', and 'The Equaliser', while the BBC axed 'Black Christmas' and 'Body Contact'.

New MORI Poll on TV VIOLENCE

Seven in ten (69 per cent) of the people in Great Britain feel that violence on television has an effect on real-life behaviour, according to the results of a MORI poll of more than 2000 adults throughout Great Britain featuring as the cover story in the October *Reader's Digest*.

Another seven in ten (69 per cent) say that terrorist organisations should never be allowed to express their views on TV, and two thirds (66 per cent) feel that TV reporting of terrorist activities strengthens the status of terrorists.

Seventy-one per cent feel that the behaviour of many children is adversely affected by television. *The Reader's Digest* article stresses the importance of this concern, in view of the calculation that the average child could witness some 16,000 violent deaths on TV by his or her late teens.

KEYWORDS

The following Keyword is used in this Unit. Make sure you have understood what it means.

pressure group

Q UESTIONS

1. When was the 'Clean Up TV' Campaign started?
2. What has it achieved during its first twenty-five years?

Q UESTIONS

1. What was the main finding of the MORI poll on TV violence?
2. What do people feel about the link between TV and terrorism?
3. Why are there fears about the effects of TV on children?
4. Which programmes were withdrawn because they contained scenes of violence?
5. Why do the producers of *EastEnders* get full marks from National VALA?

THREAT TO DEMOCRACY: PRESSURE OR TERROR?

The crash of the Pan-Am jumbo jet on Lockerbie in Scotland in 1988 was caused by a bomb placed on the plane by unknown terrorists. This extreme type of violent protest caused the deaths of 270 people.

In 1984, a bomb blew up part of the Grand Hotel in Brighton during the Conservative Party Conference. Five people were killed and thirty were injured. This incident, carried out by a group aiming to remove British Government influence in Northern Ireland, presented a serious threat to democracy since many more members of the elected Government could have been killed and removed from power. Indeed, the continuing murders of local politicians by various opposing groups of extremists creates further problems in establishing a widely acceptable system of democratic government in Northern Ireland itself. These are extreme examples of how far some individuals or groups may go to oppose a decision with which they strongly disagree.

While many **protest** groups or **pressure** groups keep within the law, there are occasions when the actions of such groups go outside the law and become illegal. Also, small groups or individuals within protest groups may decide to carry out illegal acts to further their cause even if the main group to which they belong opposes such illegal acts.

Protest in Parliament

Even within Parliament itself, some protests by individual MPs may break the rules of the House of Commons or the House of Lords. There have been several examples of MPs getting into trouble in Parliament for various reasons. Two much publicised incidents involved the picking up of the Mace (the symbol of the Speaker's authority in the House of Commons). In these cases both MPs were disciplined by the Speaker of the House of Commons.

Keeping the House in order

THE furore sparked by Ron Brown's fumble-fingered exhibition of mace-twirling has turned up the pressure for stiffer penalties against disruptive MPs.

The affair has highlighted what MPs on both sides of the House see as a gathering spate of loutishness which, if allowed to continue, will reduce the Commons to chaos and farce with increasing frequency...

Of the 25 recorded expulsions since the war, 15 have occurred since 1980, the majority since the start of Mrs Thatcher's third term.

The rising curve is said to represent the increasing frustration of an Opposition powerless to change the course of the Government's legislative steamroller.

(source: *The Scotsman*, 22 April 1988.)

Illegal protest: poll tax

For some people, protesting about a decision may bring them into conflict with the **law**. In the late 1980s, for example, several people, including MPs, local councillors, and members of the public objected strongly to the introduction, by the Government, of a Community Charge (Poll Tax) to replace domestic Rates as one of the ways of funding local government. Some people refused to sign the register of names for the Community Charge, while, by 1990, almost one million people in Scotland had refused to pay the money, although fines and sale of household property were threatened. In 1990 anti-poll tax marches took place in several British cities. In Glasgow, for example, 30 000 people marched in protest, while on the same weekend a similar protest in London by about 100 000 marchers ended in violent clashes between the demonstrators and the police. Some protests may be a direct threat to democracy. In 1988, for example, poll tax protesters in Edinburgh entered the Lothian Regional Council meeting room, refused to leave, and caused the Council meeting to be abandoned.

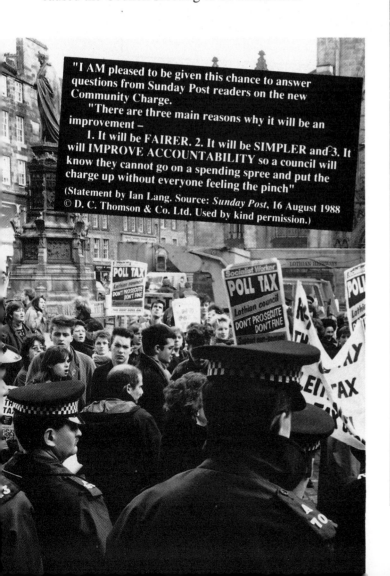

"I AM pleased to be given this chance to answer questions from Sunday Post readers on the new Community Charge.

"There are three main reasons why it will be an improvement –

1. It will be FAIRER. 2. It will be SIMPLER and 3. It will IMPROVE ACCOUNTABILITY so a council will know they cannot go on a spending spree and put the charge up without everyone feeling the pinch"

(Statement by Ian Lang. Source: *Sunday Post*, 16 August 1988 © D. C. Thomson & Co. Ltd. Used by kind permission.)

Community Charge (Poll Tax) for beginners

Britain's new local-tax system takes effect from April 1989 in Scotland, and from 1990 in England and Wales. Here is how it will work:

Some basic questions

What Is The Poll Tax?
The poll tax, or community charge as it is sometimes called, is a flat rate tax on adults. In other words, everyone in a local area receives the same bill no matter how much they earn or what they own. In Scotland, the poll tax comes into effect on 1 April 1989 and replaces the current system of domestic rates.

Will I Be Affected?
Almost definitely yes. The general exceptions will be the severely mentally handicapped, convicted prisoners, patients in long term residential homes, foreign diplomats and 18 year olds for whom Child Benefit is payable.

For everyone else, whatever your income, whatever your circumstances, whether or not you previously paid rates you will receive a poll tax bill.

(source: Edinburgh District Council. 1988)

Your support helps Greenpeace to get results

AGAINST CHEMICAL POLLUTION

A fountain of dangerous filth sprays our campaigners as they block the discharge pipe of a lead and zinc mine. The pipe was discharging thousands of tonnes of mining waste containing a large concentration of heavy metals.

AGAINST KILLING WHALES

Greenpeace campaigners get between an Icelandic whaler and the hunted whales. Our activists have boarded whaling ships — and have even fastened themselves to the anchor chains.

AGAINST KILLING SEALS

Greenpeace campaigners spray seals with harmless dyes to make the pelts worthless. They are arrested by Canadian authorities who arrive by helicopter.

AGAINST RADIOACTIVE WASTE

Two barrels of nuclear waste are dropped onto a Greenpeace inflatable, destroying the boat. Each barrel weighs a tonne.

AGAINST NUCLEAR WEAPONS

A similar banner to this was also hung from Big Ben. Earlier we had campaigned in the USSR; after our vessel Sirius had released balloons in Leningrad, the authorities towed her from her mooring.

AGAINST ACID RAIN

A montage photograph. Across Europe, the banners on pollution — causing chimneys give the message STOP ACID RAIN. In Czechoslovakia, the militia fired on our campaigners as they scaled the chimney.

In some situations protesters may feel that not enough attention is being paid to their views. If they feel their views are not being represented they may turn to illegal methods to demonstrate their anger. This can be a threat to democracy in that the protesters, who believe they have a just cause, do not accept the views of the majority.

The Royal Society for the Prevention of Cruelty to Animals (RSPCA) tries to prevent animals being treated badly. However, some people claim that RSPCA is not doing enough to end fox-hunting and animal experiments. They wish to see more direct action taken. Sometimes this direct action may involve illegal trespassing to lay false trails for fox-hounds, or it may mean breaking into premises to release animals used in experiments. Some people who claim to support Animal Rights sometimes take more violent action. In recent years some large stores have had their buildings attacked because these stores sell fur coats.

The protests of environmental groups such as Greenpeace may sometimes lead to violence and law-breaking when groups clash with the authorities during demonstrations.

Animal rights

Well, do animals have rights? What I am driving at is that the process of attributing 'rights' to individuals or animals is really about attributing priorities. It is about ordering the world in which we live, making conscious decisions about the relative values which we place on people, animals and possessions. It is not about establishing facts or establishing ultimate truths.

If animals do have rights then I have to admit that I don't know what they are. What I am clear about is my version of 'the-way-the-world-should-be'. And it does not include the callous exploitation of animals for human profit or pleasure, nor for the pursuit of scientific progress.

(source: *Green Scotland*, winter 1987/88.)

Violent protest: terrorism

Terrorism is usually a form of violent protest by a minority against a government. The violence may take a variety of forms – shootings, car-bombs, and hi-jackings. The protesters may be small groups or individuals or they may be fairly large political minorities who believe they cannot get political changes by democratic methods.

In Northern Ireland, where several groups feel they are not being represented, violence and protest are often linked. Strong objections to decisions taken by the British Government which affect Northern Ireland can lead to bitter complaints by different groups – religious, national and political. The 'problems of Ulster' have continued for a long time and much of the hatred and resentment caused by years of violence can be seen in the graph illustrating the death toll in Northern Ireland.

Government reaction

The British Government has taken several measures to try to limit what it sees as 'terrorism' in Northern Ireland. Troops have been sent to Northern Ireland to help other security forces, while some groups such as the IRA (Irish Republican Army) and the UVF (Ulster Volunteer Force) have been banned. Prevention of Terrorism Acts, relating to the detention and trial of suspects, have been passed. In 1988, for example, in an attempt to limit what British Prime Minister Margaret Thatcher called the 'oxygen of publicity' for terrorist groups, further measures were announced, limiting media reporting (especially on TV) of events in Northern Ireland.

To some people, however, these actions by the Government to limit television and radio broadcasting are themselves a threat to democracy.

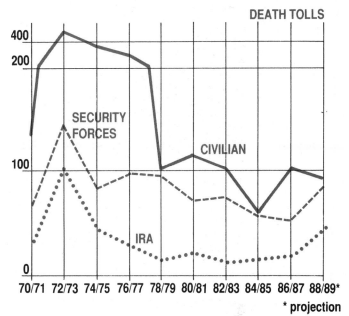

DEATH TOLLS

SECURITY FORCES

CIVILIAN

IRA

70/71 72/73 74/75 76/77 78/79 80/81 82/83 84/85 86/87 88/89*

* projection

Death toll: The number killed in the Troubles, once declining, is now increasing once more
(source: *The Observer*, 7 August 1988.)

New curbs

Sympathisers of all Ulster terrorist organisations will be included in the TV and radio interview ban being announced this afternoon by Home Secretary Douglas Hurd in the Commons.

This means supporters of banned Loyalist terror groups, as well as the IRA and their political wing Sinn Fein, will be stopped from getting their views across.

The message from Whitehall was that the Government do not differentiate between terrorists on a sectarian basis, although the ban will apply only in a Northern Ireland context.

The restrictions on interviews with members of such groups, which will not apply to newspapers, do not require legislation, so they can come into force virtually immediately.

The move has already provoked a storm of protest from politicians of all parties and from civil rights groups...

(source: *Edinburgh Evening News*, 19 October 1988.)

Laws

■ **Prevention of Terrorism (Temporary Provisions) Bill** – to empower the forfeiture of assets of those convicted of aiding terrorists. Police will get the power to investigate and freeze accounts through which terrorist money moves and banks and building societies will have to alert police if they are suspicious. The target of the Bill is funding for terrorists by superficially legitimate businesses ranging from hotels to estate agents.

■ **Elected Authorities (Northern Ireland) Bill** – to require all local government candidates to renounce violence. The long-heralded legislation is an attempt to stop the IRA's political wing, Sinn Fein, supporting terrorism through utterances by its elected councillors either inside or outside the council chamber.

(source: *The Scotsman*, 23 November 1988.)

75

Civil liberties

A SINISTER attack on British civil liberties, unprecedented in peacetime, is being mounted by the Government under the guise of fighting terrorism, Mr Roy Hattersley, the Shadow Home Secretary, said yesterday.

"The suggestion is that Northern Ireland is being used for a testing ground before the new authoritarianism is introduced throughout the United Kingdom," Labour's deputy leader said in a statement.

Treating Northern Ireland like that did not help the fight against terrorism, he argued. It would help terrorists to argue that Britain was the enemy of liberty and gave the Irish Republican Army and Ulster Defence Association two propaganda coups in two days.

Ministers knew that their announcements would be counter-productive. The Government was "more concerned with the illusion of action and the need to save face than it is with the real fight against terrorism and violence.

"Most sinister, they are using the specific issue of terrorism to justify an attack on our civil liberties that is unprecedented in peacetime. Genuine political discussion and dissent, which are central to our democracy, are now openly under attack."

(source: *The Scotsman*, 22 October 1988.)

QUESTIONS

1. In what way was the 1984 bombing of the Grand Hotel in Brighton a 'threat to democracy'?

2. Why might some people within pressure groups turn to more violent action?

3. Why did some people refuse to sign the Community Charge register?

4. Write a paragraph explaining how the Community Charge works.

5. Why does the quotation explaining the Community Charge refer to it as 'poll tax'?

6. What, according to Mr Ian Lang of the Scottish Office, are the benefits of the Community Charge?

7. Study the cartoon 'Poll Tax.' Can you explain, in a paragraph, what the cartoonist is trying to show?

8. Why are some people dissatisfied with the work of the RSPCA?

9. What is meant by Animal Rights?

10. Study the Greenpeace advertisement. List the items which Greenpeace opposes, and describe how it takes action against each.

11. In what ways are some of Greenpeace's actions illegal?

12. Are all illegal protests wrong?

13. In what ways are the rights of 'terrorists' being limited, with reference to Northern Ireland?

14. Why is this action being taken?

15. What problems might arise when these laws are applied?

A CTIVITIES

1. Compare the ways in which a teacher tries to prevent rules being broken in a classroom, and how the Speaker tries to prevent rules being broken in the House of Commons.

2. Discuss the views of people who support, and those who oppose, Vivisection. Consider Animal Rights and the rights of human beings.

3. In groups, discuss why the British Government has banned some groups in Northern Ireland. What are the advantages and disadvantages of these bans to the Government?

4. Study the planned protest by CND (below).

This October 15th there will be protest actions involving non-violent direct action at USAF Upper Heyford, Portsmouth Naval Base and in Scotland at Faslane Submarine Base. Faslane is the current Polaris base and is being massively extended to take the Trident submarines in the 1990's. At each gate of the base, various activities will take place:

1) Planting bulbs (bring your own); (2) Decorating the fence with streamers; photographs etc; (3) Vigil; (4) Marking the roads with whitewash (we have permission from Strathclyde Regional Council for this) (5) Blockading the base.

Of these, the only activity likely to lead to arrest is blockading the base. If you intend to take part in blockading it is vital to plan and prepare your actions beforehand as part of an Affinity Group in order to anticipate police tactics and avoid the possibility of violence.
(source: *Edinburgh CND News*, October 1988.)

5. Should the illegal action of blocking the base go ahead? Discuss, and write down your group's view.

6. Find out what the other groups think by listening to a spokesperson for each group.

7. Discuss the statement "The use of violence is always unacceptable." (Consider some historical and current examples of the use of violent protest.)

8. In what ways can the following groups use the media to put forward their views: a) the Government; b) extremists?

PART 2 CHANGING SOCIETY

1

NEEDS IN SOCIETY

OUR NEEDS

'No man is an island. . . ' is a quotation often used to show that no one can survive entirely on her or his own. The quotation could be expanded to include 'man, woman, teenager or child' because we all have a variety of basic **needs** and we cannot provide for all these needs by ourselves. This is especially true of very young children, who, as babies, are unable to provide for themselves many of the basic needs for their survival.

THE BASIC NEEDS OF A BABY

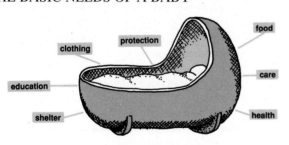

- These basic needs can be divided up into smaller, more immediate needs.

- As the baby grows up to be a young child, the basic needs remain though there are some changes in the other needs. By the time the young person is a teenager at school, these other needs have changed again.

- As people grow older many of the basic needs are similar, but there are variations in the smaller requirements, at each stage.

Baby!

Average parents can spend up to £36,000 on clothes, food, holidays, presents, and pocket money before junior reaches the age of 16.

That's according to two separate studies produced by the insurance company Legal and General and by the Family Policy Studies Centre.

And they show that a mum who gives up work to look after her family could lose as much as £135,000 in potential earnings.

BABY'S FIRST YEAR CAN EASILY COST PARENTS UP TO £1000.

First of all, there's the hardware. A cot with bedding (£150), a pram (£100), a bath (£10) or a car seat (£30) show the kind of the capital expenditure required.

Though it's often the case that grandparents and relatives will want to help by buying one or more of these big items.

Friends and relatives may help with hand-me-downs – but most new mums will try their best to have some special new things for their first baby.

They'll also want to spend about £50 giving a lick of paint and some new curtains to the nursery – even if they can't afford £300-odd on special nursery furniture.

And mum will almost certainly have had to spend some money (£100 to £150) on maternity clothes.

After all the essential items are purchased, there's baby's running costs.

Nappies, food, cotton wool and toiletries can easily add up to £50 a month...

An average baby will use up to 2000 nappies in its first year – that's 1.5 billion nappies used this year in Britain!...

(source: *Sunday Mail*, 14 August 1988.)

the average teenager

The Health Education Authority's Schools Health Education Unit, surveyed 18,002 pupils at 88 schools in Scotland, England, Wales and Northern Ireland last year to produce a detailed picture of what it is like to be aged between 11 and 16 in today's Britain.

BREAKFAST

For the typical teenager, the day starts before 8am with a light breakfast – or for as many as 20 per cent of girls and 14.4 per cent of boys no breakfast at all.

Once at school, most pupils have either a school lunch or sandwiches brought from home, although 11 per cent of 15 and 16 year old girls and 7.1 per cent of boys of the same age eat no lunch at all.

Among 16-year-olds, one in five said they were spending over £10 a week on items like records, cosmetics, soft drinks and video hire.

Q UESTIONS

1. What are the basic needs of a young baby?

2. Why is the baby unable to supply many of its own needs?

3. Write a report explaining the possible cost of looking after a baby in its first year.

4. Can you write down any other needs a baby might have, in addition to those on the list?

5. What expenses might be involved for a teenager going to: a) a disco; and b) a sports meeting, e.g. football?

A CTIVITIES

1. Form groups of four and list the needs of:
a) a baby; b) a teenager.

2. Gather newspaper and magazine cuttings and photos to illustrate:
a) the needs of a baby; b) the lifestyle of a teenager.

3. Make some drawings, illustrations, and diagrams of your own about these two topics.

4. Stick the items you have gathered on to two sheets of paper to show what you have found out about these topics.

5. Each group should give a verbal report on the investigations to the rest of the class.

People in need

For various reasons, there are many people in society who need special care and help. Young babies have already been mentioned. Other people include ill, poor, disabled, unemployed, homeless and elderly people and some other disadvantaged groups such as women and refugees.

Here and on page 79 you will see examples of some disadvantaged groups of people in the UK. Read the extracts carefully.

Children

This picture was taken recently in England.

It was not set up or reconstructed. We simply asked our photographer to record what he found in the cities of our country.

Peter is two years old.

He's just one of almost 2 million children living in appalling deprivation in Britain today.

Living in conditions that create family tensions, domestic violence and worse.

(source: *The Observer*, 20 December 1987. From The Children's Society 1985 advertising campaign. Reproduced by kind permission of The Children's Society.)

Refugees

THE Khaireh family are refugees who escaped from war-torn Somalia last year and after a short stay in London came to Scotland two months ago.

Although grateful to be safe from the civil war in their own country, in which thousands have died, they say they are finding it very difficult to settle down here.

Mr Hussein Khaireh said: "We feel very confused. No one has visited us or told us what to do and we don't really know what our rights are as refugees. We don't want to be parasites, both of us had good jobs in Somalia and I feel shame that we have to ask for help, but we don't have any choice."

(source: *Scotland on Sunday*, 9 October 1988.)

1. Describe the conditions in the photograph.

2. How many children live in 'appalling deprivation in Britain?

3. What needs does the refugee family have?

4. Why does 'life revolve round the Post Office' for many poor people?

5. Which groups of poor people are mentioned?

6. Why are there so many young homeless people in London?

7. Where do they stay?

8. Explain the disabled person's statement, "It is society that disables me."

9. List some of the ways the needs of women could be met in terms of: a) planning; b) employment.

ACTIVITIES

1. Divide into groups, and select one example of people in need. List, in one column, as many needs as you can for your selected people in need.

2. In a second column on your sheet of paper, list ways in which each of these needs could be met.

3. Collect newspaper cuttings and photographs to help illustrate your group's items.

4. Each group should tell the others what has been found out concerning 'Needs and Solutions'.

5. Discuss the particular problems to be solved to make it easier for a disabled person in a wheelchair to shop in your local shopping area.

6. Write a letter to your local councillor outlining the specific problems in the shopping area for disabled people, and how they might be solved.

The poor

NINE o'clock in the morning outside the Post Office, and the queue is already 20 yards long, even in the driving rain.

Here in Giroland, life revolves around the Post Office. Old women huddle together, cradling their pension books and the single mothers, holding their crying children at bay, search for their allowance books in amongst the lipstick and emergency plastic nappies. Middle-aged men cough and swear quietly, frequently checking that the green Giro is still in the back pocket.

As I stand in line, I'm just like everyone else, working out how much of the Giro money I have already spent, wondering which particular debt I can delay for another week, and wishing that everyone in front of me would drop dead so that I could get to the top of the queue and get my 30 quid...

(source: *The Scotsman*, 23 March 1988.)

THE HOMELESS

Centrepoint Soho, the London-based charity for homeless young people, which is 18 years old this Christmas, also produced a study this week, with £20,000 from Charity Projects. It estimates that there are 50,000 homeless young people in London.

"What's surprising is how ordinary they all are," observed one worker.

According to the survey they are at least as well educated as their housed contemporaries. Forty per cent of them have become homeless after coming to London to find work. Thirty one per cent came to the capital having being turfed out of their family home or having fled it after a row or violence...

He says that increasing numbers of young people are sleeping in tube stations or in squats and are falling prey to protection rackets.

(source: *New Statesman & Society*, 18 December 1987.)

Disabled people

A disabled person comments that disability is part of normality.

..."Normal communities contain disabled people but so far they have not been allowed to take part in those communities on an equal basis.

"I am transport disabled, not by my cerebral palsy, but by the way buses are built, driven and organised. Other people are transport disabled too, mothers with young children, old people." But, he says, rather than make it possible for disabled people to use the normal bus service, special services are provided which isolate them from the rest of the community.

(source: *Scotland on Sunday*, 13 November 1988.)

Women

THE PROBLEMS

When planners and architects overlook the women's point of view the result, says Councillor Helen Graham, is that:

● shops are sited away from bus routes and other public transport;

● mothers have to go up stairs and escalators and through narrow supermarket check-outs with pushchairs and buggies;

● children have to cross busy main roads to get to school;

● pedestrian refuge islands are too narrow for prams;

● badly-lit footpaths and subways leave unaccompanied women open to attack.

(source: *Edinburgh Evening News*, 17 January 1989.)

THE EQUAL Opportunities Commission has launched fresh targets for the 1990s to make sure women gain from their new-found importance to the economy. . . .

The key areas the EOC will focus on include:

● Pressing for adequate child care;

● Removing barriers which hinder women's training opportunities;

● Narrowing the gap between men and women's wages;

● Increasing the status of part-timers;

● Increasing fiscal and pensions equality.

(source: *The Scotsman*, 18 January 1989.)

Many groups have great difficulty in trying to improve their situation. We shall look in detail at the needs of two of these groups – unemployed people and elderly people.

Being unemployed

John MacKay lost his job a year ago as a fitter in an engineering works. Jennifer, his wife, works as a check-out supervisor in a supermarket nearby. Their children, Jayne and Jamie, are at secondary school.

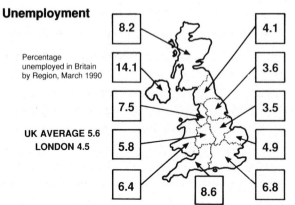

DIARY OF ONE UNEMPLOYED MAN

9.00 Got up and ate a roll with cup of tea.

9.30 Walked to Job Centre. Nothing available, again!

10.00 Went for walk in park.

11.00 Back home. Read newspaper.

12.30 Jennifer home for dinner. We argue because dinner isn't ready.

1.00 Made dinner – bread, butter, jam.

1.30 Watched T.V.

2.00 Walked to betting shop, met pal.

3.00 Back home. Tried the crossword.

3.45 Jayne and Jamie home from school. Fixed Jamie's bike.

5.15 Jennifer home from work. Have tea, fish, chips with family.

5.45 Watch T.V. (News), and read "Advertiser".

6.30 Help Jayne with homework.

7.00 Watch T.V. (Quiz show).

7.30 Gave kids some pocket money for next day. Jennifer said it was too much. Argument.

8.00 Went to pub. Bought a pint. Watch locals playing darts.

9.00 Home for supper.

10.00 Jennifer shows me a job advert in the paper. Promise to check it.

10.30 Watched old western film on T.V. till 12.00, then bed.

Unemployment has become a boring daily routine for this man. There are hundreds of thousands of unemployed people like him in many parts of Britain.

Unemployment

Percentage unemployed in Britain by Region, March 1990

8.2 4.1 14.1 3.6 7.5 3.5

UK AVERAGE 5.6
LONDON 4.5

5.8 4.9 6.4 8.6 6.8

(source: *Department of Employment*, March 1990.)

A high rate of unemployment is expensive for the country, both in terms of the large sum of Unemployment Benefit which is paid out, and also in the wastage of people's skills. Areas where there is widespread unemployment may need extra help. Businesses, shops and entertainment centres will not do well where people have no money to spend. These companies may be in danger of closing down, which would mean the loss of even more jobs.

A CTIVITIES

1. Divide into groups, discuss the unemployed man's diary, then,

a) write a diary by John assuming he had lost his job as a highly paid computer sales manager.

b) write a diary by Jennifer, assuming John has left home permanently, and Jennifer has lost her job in the supermarket.

2. Construct a graph showing the UK unemployment trend, based on the unemployment statistics of the last ten years.

THE CAUSES OF UNEMPLOYMENT

When factories, offices, and other work-places close or reduce the number of their employees, people become unemployed and need to find other jobs. There are many reasons why people lose their jobs:

LOSING YOUR JOB – WHY?

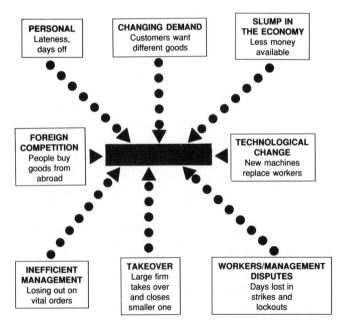

PERSONAL Lateness, days off

CHANGING DEMAND Customers want different goods

SLUMP IN THE ECONOMY Less money available

FOREIGN COMPETITION People buy goods from abroad

TECHNOLOGICAL CHANGE New machines replace workers

INEFFICIENT MANAGEMENT Losing out on vital orders

TAKEOVER Large firm takes over and closes smaller one

WORKERS/MANAGEMENT DISPUTES Days lost in strikes and lockouts

Jobs suffer body blows

Widespread redundancies announced in Scotland in the past few days were only the latest in a series of body blows to the country's industry.

"Yes, it was a bad week," said Mr. John Henry, deputy general secretary of the Scottish Trades Union Congress.

"But it is such a long time since we had a good week."

The biggest single blow came at NEI Peebles in Edinburgh where management announced the loss of another 230 jobs.

In Fife Marconi Defence Systems at Hillend were refusing to comment on redundancies among their 1000 work force.

In the west of Scotland, Rolls Royce said they were making 70 technicians redundant.

"All these add up. There is no way industry is coming into Scotland to make up for the loss of these jobs," said Mr. Henry...

(source: *Edinburgh Evening News*, 5 September 1987.)

QUESTIONS

1. What problems face someone who is unemployed?

2. What needs arise from being made unemployed?

3. Which areas in Britain are above the UK average for unemployment levels?

4. Why do you think there are differences in the unemployment levels in different parts of Britain?

5. List the places mentioned in the newspaper item, 'Jobs suffer body blows'. Beside each place indicate the number of people who have lost their jobs.

ACTIVITIES

1. Divide into groups of four and discuss where you could find information about unemployment, then write letters requesting information.

2. Arrange an interview with someone who is or has been unemployed, and prepare a questionnaire for the interview, based on 'The Needs of an Unemployed Person'.

3. Write a report based on the interview.

4. Find examples of recent closures, cut-backs, and redundancies in your area of Scotland. (Look in newspapers and magazines.)

Being elderly

Pensioner's Christmas

Tomorrow will be mainly a solitary affair for one Edinburgh pensioner – housebound with chronic bronchitis and arthritis in a cold flat with no hot water.

In the morning, a neighbour will call with the season's greetings. Then she will bolt the door against intruders and spend the day alone.

She said: "I will probably cook myself a bit of chicken."

For thousands of pensioners it is just another day in the battle against winter's cold.

Aged 69, she has been a widow for more than ten years and has a war widow's pension.

Chill

The flat she and her husband bought to be nearer medical treatment at the Royal Infirmary is urgently in need of modernisation. Dampness next to the chimney breast has caused sections of wallpaper to peel off. She wears a scarf around her head to protect herself from the chill.

The only heating in the two-apartment home, which has no bathroom and no hot water, is a gas fire which she keeps low for fear of high bills.

The house was recently insulated by Leith Insulation Project who considered it the coldest they had visited.

But she said: "I wouldn't like to shift from here. My neighbours are very good to me – I don't know what I would do without them. They do all my shopping for me and they will see that I have bread and milk to see me through the holiday.

"It's the cold and the damp I don't like. And the bills are so high. I put money aside for them each week but I have been broken into once, so I keep it here and there.

"I will lock my door tomorrow morning and it will stay like that all day. I miss my husband."

She takes medication daily and is visited each month by a district nurse. Her local doctor also calls regularly to see she is all right...

(source: *Edinburgh Evening News*, 24 December 1986.)

Not all old people live in such difficult circumstances as those described above, but large numbers of old people do need special help in a variety of ways. Many need help to understand information, for example, about filling in official forms, or about taking medicine.

5. Give a verbal report to the group of the results of your investigations.

6. Look at job advertisements in a newspaper. Find six different jobs that an unemployed person, who has no special skills, could apply for.

7. Discuss ways in which unemployed people could be helped in finding new jobs.

AGE-OLD PROBLEM

by **Nicola Barry**

MORE PEOPLE are living longer than ever before. In 1977, for instance, the average life expectancy in Britain was 72 years – almost 23 years more than the corresponding figure at the turn of the century.

In Scotland almost 14 per cent of the population are over the age of 65, more than 5 per cent being over 75. What these figures fail to show is the fact that the elderly population is itself getting progressively older.

And this trend is expected to continue, with the number of people of 85 years and over continuing to increase.

We live in an ageing society in which a large proportion of older people require continuous medication, in many cases for multiple complaints.

It is easy for them to confuse the tablets because of the number prescribed.

...Many misconceptions surround old age. One is the belief that old people are all in institutions when the vast majority, in fact, live at home. Another is the belief that it is worse to suffer – mentally or physically – when young than when old. For the elderly, suffering is no less acute.

(source: *Edinburgh Evening News*, 27 April 1987.)

NEEDS – THE ELDERLY

Over 65's in UK

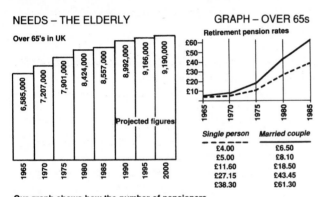

6,585,000	1965
7,207,000	1970
7,901,000	1975
8,424,000	1980
8,557,000	1985
8,992,000	1990
9,166,000	1995
9,190,000	2000

Projected figures

GRAPH – OVER 65s
Retirement pension rates

£60 £50 £40 £30 £20 £10

1965 1970 1975 1980 1985

Single person	Married couple
£4.00	£6.50
£5.00	£8.10
£11.60	£18.50
£27.15	£43.45
£38.30	£61.30

Our graph shows how the number of pensioners has risen over the years and how their pensions have increased.

(source: *The Sunday Post*, 13 November 1988.)

Many old people have difficulty moving around. Travelling, especially if elderly people have to get on and off buses, can be a problem.

The trip that spells danger
BUSES RISK TO ELDERLY

By **IAN BURRELL**

Almost half the passengers injured on buses each year in Lothian and Borders are elderly, it was revealed today.

So in a bid to reduce the risks, a poster campaign has been launched by police in conjunction with Lothian Transport Department and Eastern Scottish, urging old people to take extra care – particularly when getting on and off the vehicles.

...Elderly people should make more use of the handrails when getting on and off, standing and even when seated. Ideally they should stay on the lower deck near the exit and remain seated until the bus stops...

(source: *Edinburgh Evening News*, 24 June 1987.)

HOLD TIGHT

WATCH YOUR STEP

Many pensioners' main need is for more money, and there have been protests by some elderly people, claiming that retirement pensions are too low.

Lack-of-Lifestyle

THE elderly of Britain are neglected people. The country has more than 10,000,000 pensioners who should now be enjoying life more than ever. In most cases it is the opposite. Trying to make ends meet. A battle for survival.

News on Sunday today launches a campaign to bring home the plight of the pensioners to the government. To win them a realistic pension so that they can live with dignity. The elderly received a rise in April of 80p for a single pensioner and £1.30 for a couple, bringing pensions up to £39.50 and £63.25 respectively...

As Jack Jones, former T and GWU secretary and Age Concern vice-president, wrote in News on Sunday last week:

"Silent pain evokes no response. The pain of the elderly must be heard. The more pensioners organise themselves, the louder our voice will be heard." (source: *News on Sunday*, 16 August 1987.)

The elderly

A EUROPEAN Charter of Rights for Elderly People has been called for by David Martin, Euro MP for the Lothians.

He said that the elderly people of the European Community have substantially contributed to the wealth of the EC.

"The Community is a comparatively prosperous region," he said.

"And yet it contains a substantial number of elderly people who live in poverty."

"This situation is unacceptable and unnecessary."

But in Britain 47 per cent of families defined as "poor" are made up of elderly people. .

"There is a simple explanation for this," continued Mr Martin.

He claimed: "A German pensioner gets £125 per week from the state whereas the equivalent pension in this country is £41.15."...

The Charter would involve not only bringing British pensions up to standard with the best in Europe.... (cont.)

QUESTIONS

1. What problems faced the Edinburgh pensioner?

2. How many people in Britain are over pension age?

3. Why do you think the number of old people is increasing? (Give at least three reasons.)

4. What increased needs will there be by the year 2000?

5. What did Jack Jones (of Age Concern) say about the pensioners?

6. What advice was given by Lothian Transport to help old people on the buses?

7. Why was the advice needed?

8. What needs might be included in the Euro-Charter for the elderly?

9. Write a report, entitled, 'The Needs of the Elderly.'

ACTIVITIES

1. Divide into groups, about four people in each group, and prepare a questionnaire to find out the most pressing problems/needs of old people.

2. Interview two pensioners about their needs.

3. Give a verbal report to the class of what your group found out from the interview.

4. The item, 'Fantasy Journey', will be read to you.

5. Each group should prepare a large poster illustrating the needs and problems of elderly people. The areas of special need could be divided into:
a) housing; b) in the home; c) transport; d) shopping; e) crime. Each group could choose a different need.

6. Find out about, and give a verbal report to the class on, 'How house design and technology in the home can help old people.'

7. Arrange a visit to a retirement home to find out how the home tries to meet the needs of the elderly. Report back to the class on your visit.

Fantasy Journey

Purpose:

This exercise is intended to put you in touch with some of the feelings an elderly person may experience prior to admission to an old folk's home. It relies on you using your imagination.

Process

Shut your eyes.
Imagine yourself back in your own living-room as it is now.
Sit in your favourite chair and look around.
Remind yourself of everything that you treasure.
You have lived in this house for very many years.
Your parents are dead.
Your children have grown up. They live elsewhere.
Your partner died a few years ago.
You are 80 years old.
You are alone.
You fell and broke your hip two winters ago, and never fully recovered.
You are quite frail.
Your body doesn't do what you want it to, and this frustrates you.
You managed to cope with the help of neighbours, a Home Carer and Meals-on-Wheels, but now you can't keep going.
Today you are going to a Retirement Home to stay there permanently.
You don't expect to come back home.
You are waiting for the Social Worker to come and take you to the Home.
You think back to happy and sad memories of things that happened in the room – Christmas, Birthdays, Death.
At your feet is the suitcase in which you have put your most treasured items.
What have you put in the suitcase?
The Social Worker comes.
She picks up your case and takes you by the arm.
She wants to lock the door for you, but you don't let her.
You close the door.
You lock it.
You walk down the path.
You don't look back.

KEYWORDS

The following Keywords are used in this Unit. Make sure you have understood what they mean.

needs   **deprivation**   **disadvantaged**

WHO DO YOU DEPEND ON?

Everyone has needs. Whether people are young or old, male or female, black or white, employed or unemployed, everyone needs food, clothing and shelter. Other things are more important or less important to us depending on our individual circumstances, e.g. education, work and health care. All of us, however, need these things at some time in our lives.

Providing for these needs involves a large number of people. In the next few pages you will find examples of how we depend on others to help us to make life more bearable and comfortable, and sometimes even to survive.

Elderly people

When you feel ill you visit a doctor or ask the doctor to call at your house. The doctor's job is to try to help you or, if he or she cannot, put you in touch with someone else who can. Old people are more likely to become ill than younger people and very often they suffer from more than one illness at a time. In this case-study you will find out more about some of the people involved in caring for the elderly.

Mary Dodds (74) was found lying on the floor of her first floor Govan flat in the early hours of this morning. Police, assisted by the fire brigade, broke into the flat through a window after the alarm had been raised by a friend. Mrs Dodds, a widow living alone, had not been seen for two days and had missed her weekly visit to the local bingo hall.

An ambulance took Mrs Dodds to the Royal Infirmary where she was found to be suffering from hypothermia. A spokeswoman for the Social Work department said later that Mrs Dodds had recently been visited by a health visitor but had turned down the offer of help because she felt it would remove her independence.

A neighbour said that the old lady had recently been suffering from 'flu and her family, who lived in Inverness, were concerned that she often switched off her electric fire to save money. They were also worried that she did not spend enough on food. A hospital spokesman later confirmed that Mrs Dodds was expected to make a full recovery after a period of care and treatment in hospital. It was hoped that she could eventually return home, but in the meantime attempts were being made to find out if she could be cared for in **sheltered housing**, an old people's home or perhaps in the **geriatric ward** of a local hospital.

Q UESTIONS

1. Make a list of all the people involved when Mary Dodds became ill.
2. Why do you think she became ill?
3. Who might have helped her to avoid her problem?
4. Why did Mrs Dodds turn down the offer of help from the Social Work department?
5. Of all the people mentioned in the newspaper report who do you think has the greatest responsibility for helping Mrs Dodds?
6. How might Mrs Dodds react to the suggestion in the last sentence of the report?
7. What do you think should happen to Mrs Dodds when she leaves the hospital?

A CTIVITIES

Arrange for an interview with an elderly person, either through your teacher or by asking an elderly person you know.

Take with you to the interview some questions that you have decided in class you would like to ask the elderly person. You may want to find out what they see as the problems of being old, what their needs are and the kind of help they need. If a few of you in the class interview different elderly people you can compare the results afterwards and perhaps draw a graph to show how they answered your questions.

Remember! You must make proper arrangements for your interview, so that your interviewee knows exactly when and where to expect to see you.

ILLNESS AND OLD AGE

Hypothermia (cold) can be a killer for elderly people. If they do not keep themselves warm enough their body temperature may get so low that they become very weak and their body stops working properly. Sometimes they go into a deep coma and die. Often they survive, but because they are so weak they catch other diseases, such as **pneumonia**. Other diseases which affect many old people are **heart disease, arthritis, rheumatism**

and **bronchitis**. About 30 per cent of elderly people in Britain suffer from some kind of chronic illness or physical handicap, and many old people suffer from more than one illness at a time. When old people do become ill they take much longer to recover than younger people.

Old people are more likely to have accidents in the home.

Many old people die in the winter months, often because they do not have enough money to spend on food and heating. This highlights another need which elderly people have – the need for money to pay for the necessities of life.

A CTIVITIES

Using encyclopaedias and dictionaries available in the classroom or in the school library, find out more about the diseases which affect old people. Then find out how these can be avoided.

MOST OF Mrs Nong's day is spent moving restlessly between the television set and the sitting room window of the Edinburgh council house where she lives with her son and daughter-in-law and their family. She is 81 years old, living out her old age in a country a whole world away from her homeland of Vietnam and she still seems as little at ease in her new country as when she arrived here eight years ago.

There are reckoned to be 300 or more elderly Chinese or Vietnamese people like Mrs Nong living in and around Edinburgh, isolated by their lack of English and lack of motivation to assimilate anything of the British way of life. To help break down this isolation, Shun Au, community education worker at the Roundabout International Centre in Leith, is planning to start a lunch and social club for them.

Ordinary lunch clubs are unsuitable for the Chinese and elderly Vietnamese, he explains. "They could not eat the food or communicate with the others there. And they cannot join in any kind of entertainment that is provided because they simply wouldn't understand what was going on."

(source: *The Scotsman*, 16 February 1988.)

Q UESTIONS

1. How does Mrs Nong spend her day?
2. Why does she still seem as little at ease as when she arrived here eight years ago?
3. What plans are there to help elderly Chinese and Vietnamese people in Edinburgh?
4. Why do the elderly Chinese and Vietnamese people not join ordinary lunch clubs?

WHO CAN HELP?

Family and Community

The most important people in many elderly people's lives are their family, friends and neighbours. In many cases they give the support which old people need. By giving attention and visiting they help to reduce the **boredom** and **loneliness** which can be a problem for the elderly.

The activities which are available in the local **community** are also very important for old people. Bowling centres, bingo, church activities, coffee mornings, lunch clubs and many other other activities give the elderly an opportunity to meet other people and chat about the ordinary things of life. The more an elderly person is involved in some kind of community activity the less chance there is of becoming lonely. This can also be very important for people who have recently retired – the change from having a daily job where they are active and meet people to having a lot of time on their hands can be very difficult for some people to cope with. Some colleges run courses to help elderly people to plan what they will do with the time. Sometimes, however, the elderly people in Britain are left to fend for themselves. British people are not as good as people in some other European and many Asian countries at giving proper care and attention to elderly relatives.

Q UESTIONS

1. How can the family help its older members?
2. What activities in the community help the elderly?
3. Why do recently retired people need help?

Be A Good Neighbour

...At this time of year it's vital that we don't forget our elderly friends and relatives. If you have an elderly neighbour, living alone, then watch-out for the tell-tale signs which can often mean something is wrong.

For instance, if curtains remain drawn throughout the day, or bottles of milk remain on the doorstep, or quite simply you haven't seen them for a couple of days, then pop round to see if everything's all right.

More often than not it is, but at this time of year you could be doing your elderly relative or neighbour a real service just by showing you care and by talking to them, because remember that for people living alone Christmas can often be very lonely and depressing.

This year show you care – *be a good neighbour*.

(source: *The Selkirk Weekender*, 5 November 1988.)

Local Authority services

All Regional Councils in Scotland provide a range of useful services for elderly people. These are usually provided by the Social Work department. The most common ones are:

- Home carers
- Meals-on-Wheels
- Day centres and social clubs
- Reduced fares on public transport
- Mobile libraries
- Residential homes

A CTIVITY

Find out more about these and other services provided by the local council by collecting free leaflets from the Social Work department or your local advice centre.

Central Government services

The Government also tries to meet the needs of the elderly by providing a range of services. Some of the most important are as follows:

- **State retirement pension** (Old Age Pension) – from age 60 for a woman and age 65 for a man if retired from a regular job and if National Insurance contributions have been paid.
- **Supplementary pension** (Income Support) – For people who don't have enough money to live on and have only a small amount of savings.
- **Housing Benefit** – For people who can't afford their rent and rates.
- **Free NHS prescriptions** – Those receiving Income Support also receive free dental treatment and help with fares to hospital.

It might be thought that with all this help available there should be no problem in meeting the needs of the elderly in the 1990s. Yet many old people live in **poverty** or near-poverty. Why? Part of the answer is that the levels of payments made are too low. Another part of the answer is that many old people are reluctant to claim all the benefits and help to which they are entitled – they don't want to be seen as 'spongers', or to be accepting 'charity'.

A CTIVITIES

1. Plan and draw your own diagram to show the needs of elderly people. Beside each need which you have identified write an example of the kind of help which is available to help meet this need.

2. In groups, discuss the ideas in the final paragraph above. Write a group report on why, in spite of all the help which seems to be available to elderly people, many still live in poor conditions and are unhappy. Report back to the whole class, then discuss your findings as a class.

THE 'WOOPIES'!

Advertisers, holiday companies and marketing people have discovered a new breed of pensioner – the **'Woopies'**. The term stands for 'Well Off Older People' and there are increasing numbers of them about. They are the elderly people who can afford more **luxuries** in their retirement. They may spend the winter months sunning themselves in the Costa Brava or the Algarve, far from the cold and wet of the British winter. The Government may in future treat these pensioners differently from pensioners on low incomes by removing their right to some free treatment under the NHS. The Government has said that it may target help towards the poorer pensioners. This means, however, that it will first have to find out who these poorer pensioners are by kind of **'means test'**, which would be very unpopular.

Glams making Woopie

JOHN BURROWES on how Scotland's affluent oldsters are making their presence felt.

BRITAIN'S newest group-price organisation says it has been over-whelmed by the number of Scots 'Glams' and 'Woopies' who have inquired about membership with them.

For the 'Glams' – Greying, Leisured, Affluent and Married – and the 'Woopies' – Well Off Older People – are the emerging affluent in society. And now, under the management cover of the Association of Retired Persons, founded just three months ago, they are using their numbers to win cut-price deals in insurance, hotel bookings and holidays...

Many big companies and organisations have been actively pursuing the Glams market long before ARP got the idea of group-pricing for them. For, despite the obvious numbers of over-50s who are neither Glam nor Woopie, there is a growing number in that age group with money to spend.

Recent figures show that the over-55s have between them almost 40 per cent of the net wealth of the country...

Builders, holiday firms, insurance companies and others aware of the figures are actively pursuing them more than before. Thomson Holidays have challenged Saga, the over-55s holiday specialists, with a variety of packages to suit the blue and pink rinses...

(source: *The Observer (Scotland)*, 4 December 1988.)

GETTING THERE CHEAPER!

Once you reach 60, the Senior Citizen Railcard is your passport to better value rail travel.

Full details and application form in Senior Citizen Railcard leaflet available from all principal stations and Rail Appointed Travel Agents.

Senior Citizen Railcard

Q UESTIONS

1. Who are (a) the 'Glams', and (b) the 'Woopies'?

2. Why are many big companies and organisations interested in these groups?

3. What special benefits are available for 'Woopies' and 'Glams'?

4. Why does the Government want to remove some of their NHS benefits?

Unemployed people

Becoming unemployed or being unable to find a job is something which everybody dreads. A job brings in a wage or salary and with it the ability to buy the **necessities** of life – food, clothes, a roof over your head – and some of the luxuries – entertainment, holidays, household gadgets. Life 'on the dole' is much more difficult.

For many people in today's world, being jobless is something they will have to cope with at some time in their life.

WHAT DO UNEMPLOYED PEOPLE NEED?

Most people without jobs have the same needs as those who are in employment – necessities and some luxuries. The Government helps by providing Unemployment Benefit and other financial assistance, but this is unlikely to be enough to allow families to enjoy the same kind of **lifestyle** or standard of living as that of families earning wages.

The most important needs of the unemployed are shown in the diagram.

WHAT DO THEY NEED?

A JOB

£££
TO SATISFY NEEDS
e.g. food
shelter
clothing
some luxuries

EDUCATION OR RETRAINING

WHO CAN HELP?

The problem of unemployment is such a big one for the country that the only way to solve or at least reduce it is to attack it on a nationwide scale. The Government, in addition to providing money, has introduced a number of ways of trying to help unemployed people get back to work. Here are some of those ways.

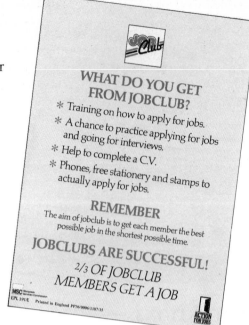

Restart—a course to help you find a job.

The course will help with:
- successful job hunting
- tackling applications
- getting replies
- seeing your strengths and skills
- finding out about other jobs you could do
- finding out what other help is available
- benefits while you are out of work

Who can apply?
You can apply if you are over 18 years and have been out of work for more than 6 months

How will it affect benefits?
You will continue to receive Unemployment Benefit or Supplementary Allowances on existing rules and you can sign early if the course falls in a week when you normally sign on.

Where is the course and what about fares?
Courses are held locally and you will be able to reclaim full travel expenses. Tea or coffee will be supplied.

How long does the course last?
The course lasts 5 days. On some courses you may be able to continue for one day each week for up to 6 weeks.

How to apply
Your jobcentre can give you an application form and arrange the dates of your course. They can also answer your questions about Restart Courses.

Leaving school at 16 or 17?

YTS provides training and planned work experience for up to two years to equip young people for working life.

YTS gives 16-year-olds **two** years of training and 17-year-olds one year, with special arrangements for young people with disabilities and some other groups.

The two-year programme involves at least 20 weeks off-the-job training (for example in a college or training centre) in addition to on-the-job training and planned work experience. Every trainee is given the opportunity to take or work towards a recognised vocational qualification.

Financial help

Sixteen-year-old entrants receive a basic tax-free allowance of £29.50 a week in their first year, increasing to £35 in their second year. Those joining on a one-year entitlement receive a basic £29.50 for the first three months and £35 for the other nine months. In particular circumstances some non-employed trainees will receive help with travel costs and lodgings.

A range of grants is available to employers and organisations who become YTS providers.

Who is eligible?

1. To participate
All 16- and 17-year-olds, with special arrangements for young people with disabilities and certain other groups.

2. To run a training scheme
Public and private employers, local authorities, voluntary bodies, training organisations, chambers of commerce and similar concerns who offer training of the required standard.

3. To provide work experience
There is wide scope for employers of all sizes in all industries to provide planned work experience for YTS trainees.

Contact
Your local Careers Office or Jobcentre. Employers should contact their nearest Training Commission Area Office (see page 34).

Interested in starting your own business?

Start-up training for small business.

The *Business Enterprise Programme* (BEP) offers seven days of training, normally spread over five weeks, in the skills needed to run a small business. BEP courses provide training in such subjects as finance, marketing, legal requirements, management and business planning, which lead to the development of a business plan. By the end of a BEP course you will be able to consider self-employment realistically and assess the likely success of your individual business idea.

There are BEP courses aimed specifically at the needs of those starting up in business in different sectors, like catering and retailing. Mini-BEP courses lasting up to two days are also available and there is an open learning BEP package for those who are unable to attend courses.

Who is eligible?

You can take part in a BEP course whether you are currently employed or not. BEP courses are free.

If you are unemployed, you can join BEP within Employment Training and you do not have to have been unemployed for six months (see pages 16–17).

For graduates who are interested in becoming self-employed and for training for the owner/managers of new and existing small businesses, see page 18.

Contact
Your local Jobcentre.

Some of these schemes are designed to help young school leavers, others are for unemployed adults. Some are designed for the long-term unemployed, some for people who have only recently been made redundant. There are special schemes for people with disabilities or long-term health problems and for people who want to start up their own businesses.

Only a few of the Government's many schemes to help the unemployed are shown here. You can find out about the others by visiting your nearest Jobcentre where there is a large variety of leaflets describing them in detail.

BUT IS ALL THIS EFFORT WORTHWHILE?

Here is what the Secretary of State for Employment (the person in the Government whose job is to help the unemployed) said in 1988 when he launched a new 'Training for Employment' scheme:

Introduction by Norman Fowler, Secretary of State for Employment

Over the past 18 months, unemployment has fallen by nearly 600,000. At the same time, hundreds of thousands of jobs have been created in many sectors of our economy.

One of the most crucial tasks facing this country is to ensure that unemployed people, particularly those who have been out of work for more than six months, are given every help to take full advantage of the growing number of job vacancies. However, many unemployed people lack the skills they need to compete for jobs.

The White Paper "Training for Employment" sets out our strategy for meeting this challenge. It announces a major new programme – aimed at giving unemployed people the skills and confidence they need to take up the opportunities now open to them.

The new programme will have annual resources of about £1.4 billion from the Government. It will also draw in substantial resources from employers. Through this partnership the new programme will enable some 600,000 people to be trained each year.

It will provide a wide range of high quality training to meet individual needs. It represents one of the most massive training initiatives ever undertaken by any Government here or abroad – a major commitment by the Government to help unemployed people to get back to work.

Norman Fowler

Some people do not agree with this view however. The Labour Party believes that the Government figures do not tell the truth about how high unemployment really is. Labour MPs say that it is much higher and that the Government's schemes are not doing much to give people 'real' jobs. The trades unions decided in 1988 that they could not support the new training programme because it did not provide a real solution to the huge problem of unemployment.

EMPLOYMENT TRAINING - THE ARGUMENTS AGAINST

1. The scheme is under-funded by the Government. More money is needed to make it effective.
2. Payments to people on the scheme are too low - only £10 in addition to Income Support.
3. The training period is too short. Six months does not allow people any proper training – at least two years' training is needed to learn real skills.
4. The training is low-quality: people finish the training without having learned skills or completed courses leading to qualifications.

QUESTIONS

1. Choose one of the schemes introduced by the Government to help people find work. Describe the kind of help it offers to unemployed people.
2. Why does the Secretary of State for Employment think that Employment Training (ET) is important?
3. What arguments are put forward by people opposed to ET?
4. How important do you think ET might be?

Unemployed people need jobs which will be permanent and which will not lead again to 'the dole' within a few months or years. The following table shows the kinds of jobs which will be available in the years towards 2000 and the kinds of jobs which are likely to become less important:

TOMORROW'S JOBS IN SCOTLAND

	Employment Levels (000s)						%Change		
	1981 (actual)			2001 (est.)			1981-2001		
MORE JOBS	M	F	T	M	F	T	M	F	TOTAL
Science, Engineering & Technology Profess.	77	7	84	122	18	140	58.4	142.9	66.7
Security & Protective Services	49	5	54	78	11	89	59.2	120.0	64.8
Other Professions	59	18	77	82	32	114	39.0	77.8	48.1
Managerial	138	39	177	168	59	227	21.7	51.3	28.2
Catering, Cleaning & Personal Services	46	205	251	56	264	320	21.7	28.8	27.5
Education, Welfare & Health Professions	64	134	198	76	176	252	18.8	31.3	27.3
Clerical & related	76	244	320	76	299	375	0.0	22.5	17.2
Selling	49	91	140	46	106	152	−6.1	16.5	8.6
FEWER JOBS									
Painting, assembling, inspecting, packaging & Related	42	33	75	25	23	48	−40.5	−30.3	−36.0
Farming, Fishing & Related	45	4	49	34	4	38	−24.4	0.0	−24.4
Materials processing; making & repairing	337	63	400	260	49	309	−22.8	−22.2	−22.8
Construction, mining & Related	77	0	77	61	2	63	−20.8	+	−18.2
Transport, materials moving & storing & Related	139	8	147	122	9	131	−12.2	−12.5	−10.9
Other	50	12	62	33	15	48	−34.0	12.0	−22.6

(Source: THE SCOTTISH COUNCIL for DEVELOPMENT & INDUSTRY)

QUESTIONS

1. Which two groups of jobs are expected to grow fastest between now and 2001?
2. Which two groups are expected to show the biggest job losses?
3. Compare the list of expanding jobs with those which are expected to decline. What does this tell you about the qualifications needed by school leavers and other workers in the future?

Hitching a ride to find work abroad

...This morning 17-year-old Eoin MacKinnon from Livingston... is packing and will head for the A1 to hitch a lift to Dover and then on to Spain to look for a job and a home.

The teenager is not preparing for a trip-of-a-lifetime or in search of excitement, he simply has no reason to stay in Scotland.

Eoin is just one of thousands of Scottish teenagers who have been left penniless by the ending of the £15 a week bridging allowance.

He fears his landlord will throw him out and he can no longer rely on friends for loans and hand outs.

He said: "What hope of a future do I have if I stay here? I have tried to get a job or a YTS but at 17 I am too old for many placements and too young for casual bar work which seems to be the only other option.

"Being told that I am not entitled to any money is a bombshell. I don't know if things will be any different in Spain, but at least it'll be warm enough to sleep on the beach and begging is not looked down on there."

Eoin's tale is typical. Thrown out by his mother when just 16 and left to a life of hostels and sleeping rough until he found his present home in a flat in Edinburgh, he now has nowhere to turn.

Project workers at Edinburgh's young person's hostel, Stopover, will spend today attempting to persuade Eoin not to leave.

A worker said: "It is a desperate situation for these teenagers and what we can we tell them? There is no money for them unless they can argue that they are severe hardship cases, but to be honest the chances of being included under that category are minimal."

(source: *Scotland on Sunday*, 6 November 1988.)

QUESTIONS

1. Give two reasons why Eoin is leaving Scotland.
2. Why did he choose to go to Spain?
3. What has happened to Eoin during the last year?
4. How can teenagers like him make more money?

THE SOCIAL EFFECTS OF UNEMPLOYMENT

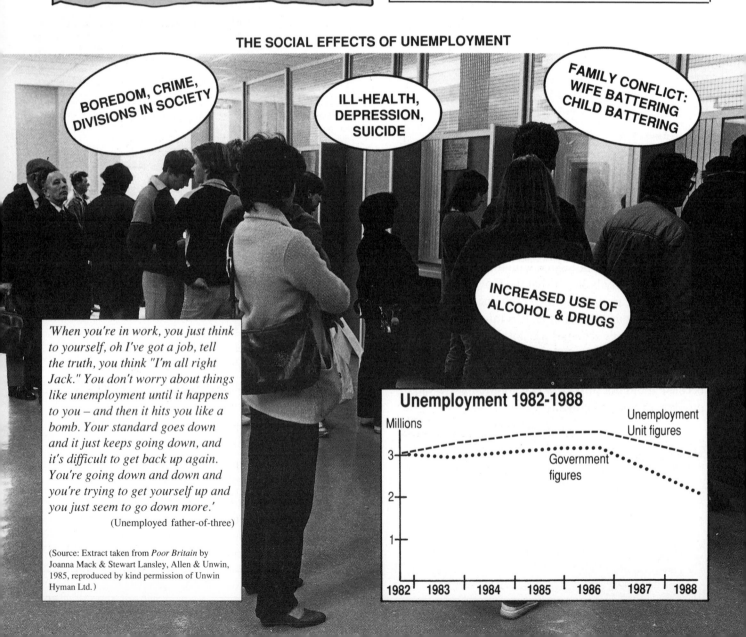

BOREDOM, CRIME, DIVISIONS IN SOCIETY

ILL-HEALTH, DEPRESSION, SUICIDE

FAMILY CONFLICT: WIFE BATTERING CHILD BATTERING

INCREASED USE OF ALCOHOL & DRUGS

'When you're in work, you just think to yourself, oh I've got a job, tell the truth, you think "I'm all right Jack." You don't worry about things like unemployment until it happens to you – and then it hits you like a bomb. Your standard goes down and it just keeps going down, and it's difficult to get back up again. You're going down and down and you're trying to get yourself up and you just seem to go down more.'

(Unemployed father-of-three)

(Source: Extract taken from *Poor Britain* by Joanna Mack & Stewart Lansley, Allen & Unwin, 1985, reproduced by kind permission of Unwin Hyman Ltd.)

Unemployment 1982-1988

Millions

Unemployment Unit figures

Government figures

3

2

1

1982 1983 1984 1985 1986 1987 1988

Subtractions in count difficult to add up

FOR THE LAST six years, the Government has systematically changed the way the unemployment statistics have been compiled.

There is now even a dispute as to how many changes the Government has actually made.

The Department of Employment owns up to six, while the Unemployment Unit, which specialises in analysing the figures, says the number is 24.

It is significant that any changes the Government has made have always resulted in the headline total of unemployment coming down...

Meanwhile the Unemployment Unit, a think-tank receiving some Government money but funded largely by charities, argues that had the way in which the figures were compiled remained unchanged, they should now be 2,956,100 – a staggering 837,300 higher.

There is no disagreement on the fact that the economy is growing and unemployment is coming down – from where, is the centre of the dispute...

Yesterday's changes, which remove all school-leavers aged 16-18 from the count, are estimated to have cut the total by about 80,000. (**Tom McGhie**) (source: *The Scotsman*, 18 November 1988.)

The diagram on page 90 shows some of the effects of unemployment on people. Many are able to cope reasonably well with the effects of losing their job or, in the case of young people, being unable to find any job at all. But others suffer in different ways depending on their own personal situation and their own strengths and weaknesses. Family and community support is also very important to unemployed people.

UNEMPLOYMENT RATES IN BRITAIN

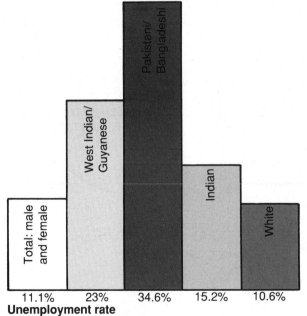

Source: Labour Force Survey, 1984

QUESTIONS

1. Between 1982 and 1988, how many changes were made in the way unemployment statistics are counted?
2. Why do the Government's unemployment figures not agree with those of the Unemployment Unit?
3. What change did the Government make in 1988?
4. Why do you think it made this change?

QUESTIONS

1. Which group has the lowest unemployment rate in Britain?
2. Within the non-white groups, which group has
   (a) the highest and
   (b) the lowest unemployment rate?

KEYWORDS

The following Keywords are used in this Unit. Make sure you have understood what they mean.

necessities	community
luxuries	'Woopies'
lifestyle	'Glams'
sheltered housing	means test
geriatric	benefit
new enties	

WHO'S RESPONSIBLE?

A welfare society

The problem of how best to care for poor people and those in need has been a problem throughout the history of human society. Before the twentieth century most people in need in Britain were looked after by their families or by their community. When times became difficult there could be widespread suffering, as in the nineteenth century when a major potato famine in Ireland led to the deaths of around a million people over a period of five years. Unemployment or old age could bring severe hardship to most people. Of course sometimes rich people or charities – often run by the Church – would help in caring for the needy.

The twentieth century has seen a change in how Britain as a society cares for those in need. This has come about through the setting up of a **welfare society** where the State, acting through central government and local authorities, provides levels of care for all people. This is known as the **Welfare State** and a basic **principle** of the Welfare State is that all citizens are entitled to these levels of care as a **right** and not as a charity. Another important principle is that people are entitled to a good education, housing, and health care according to their needs, not according to how much they can pay.

We all contribute to these welfare provisions through our **taxes** and through paying **National Insurance** contributions when we are working. Just as you can insure your house or car against fire or theft, so through National Insurance you insure yourself and your family against hardship when you cannot work because of illness, unemployment or old age.

Some benefits and services such as state education and the **National Health Service** are available to everyone. Some benefits depend upon having paid National Insurance. The old age pension and unemployment benefit come into this category. Other benefits are paid if people have a low level of income or certain types of disabilities, which will qualify them to help. These are known as **means-tested benefits**.

It was upon these principles that the Welfare State was built and the aim was to provide all citizens with a full range of benefits and services which would protect and provide for them 'from the cradle to the grave'.

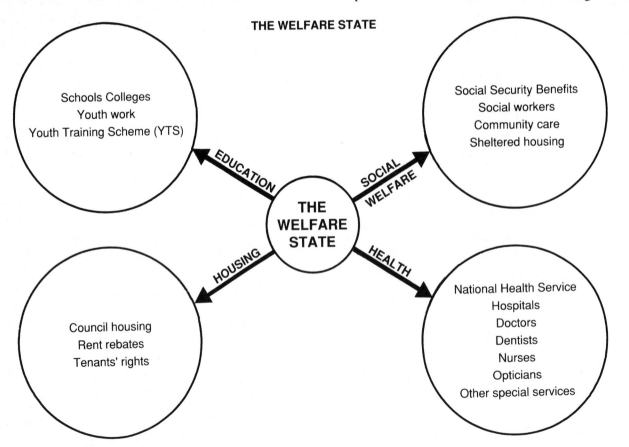

THE WELFARE STATE

Schools Colleges
Youth work
Youth Training Scheme (YTS)

Social Security Benefits
Social workers
Community care
Sheltered housing

EDUCATION

SOCIAL WELFARE

THE WELFARE STATE

HOUSING

HEALTH

Council housing
Rent rebates
Tenants' rights

National Health Service
Hospitals
Doctors
Dentists
Nurses
Opticians
Other special services

Types of benefits and levels of benefits are frequently changed. The Department of Social Security (DSS) publishes a variety of free pamphlets and booklets. These pamphlets are available from your local Social Security Office (listed in the telephone book under Social Security). Some pamphlets are also available at your local Post Office. You might be able to find a general guide to DSS benefits called *Which Benefit?* (Ref. FB2) or you may find specific booklets available for different groups of people. Among these are:

Babies and Benefits (FB8)
Bringing up Children (FB27)
Sick or Disabled (FB28)
Unemployed (FB9)
Young People's Guide to Social Security (FB23)
Retiring (FB6)

Find out from leaflets such as these who is entitled to receive the benefits listed below and the amount of money currently available for each benefit. The Contents Page on the leaflets will help you.
a) Maternity Allowance
b) Child Benefit
c) Unemployment Benefit
d) Sickness Benefit
e) Income Support
f) Family Credit
g) Retirement Pension

The future of the Welfare State

Today the Welfare State is a distinct and important feature of British society. It employs many people. It is the largest user of Government money and its activities reach into many areas of our life.

There are, however, differing views about the future of the Welfare State and about the type of welfare or caring society we should have in Britain as we approach the twenty-first century. There are many views and theories about this topic but we can separate these into two options or alternatives for the future of our Welfare State. Here is a series of statements linked with each of these two options.

Option One

The Welfare State has done an excellent job in removing from people the fear of poverty and the fear of being in need. We should improve and build upon these services and benefits.

• Everyone should be entitled to basic levels of care, of housing, health and education as a right.

• It is wrong for people to make a profit out of caring for others.

Everyone has a right to the best welfare services, no matter how poor or how wealthy they are.

• Those who earn most should pay most in taxes to help those most in need.

• Britain was among the first countries to set up a Welfare State. Some other countries, such as Sweden, have developed welfare provision well beyond the level of services in Britain. We need to spend more to improve and build upon the services we currently provide.

• Encouraging private welfare services such as schools and hospitals leads only to good services for the rich and poorer services for the less well-off.

• People should be encouraged to care for others. Families and the community have a part to play in helping those in need but only the State can make sure that all people are equally provided for.

- The Welfare State has grown too large and has taken over too many areas of people's lives. People are not encouraged to look after themselves because they feel the State will do it for them.

- Many people are poor because they lack the will-power to escape from poverty by working hard. People should be encouraged to stand on their own two feet more and look after themselves.

- State benefits should be greatly reduced or even stopped in some cases. The State should provide welfare services but only for the poorest and those most in need. State benefits should be set at the lowest possible level to act as a 'safety net' for those who genuinely need help. If State benefits are too high, then the Welfare State is only encouraging scroungers. State benefits should be means-tested to make sure that only those people who are genuinely poor are helped.

- Since they have no competition, State services are inefficient and take away from the public the freedom of choice. With more private services people would have a wider choice of more efficient services.

- People are entitled to save up and spend their own money on private hospitals or private schools rather than on holidays or new cars if they so wish.

- You cannot have a caring society when only the State looks after the needy. Individuals, families and communities need to be encouraged more to take on the caring role that the State has taken away from people.

A CTIVITY

Divide into groups of four. Choose two statements from each of the two lists concerning the future of the Welfare State. Each group will have four statements. Each person in the group should then choose or be given one statement and he or she should then spend five minutes writing down his/her ideas on this point of view. The group should then discuss in what ways the Welfare State should develop.

At the end of the discussion each group should write a brief summary of the main points raised and a spokesperson for each group should report back to the whole class for a general debate on this topic.

Housing elderly people

The debate about how best to care for people in need can be looked at more closely by examining those areas where the Welfare State (local and central government services), private companies, and charities or voluntary groups are all involved. One of these areas concerns caring for and housing elderly people. Local authorities, private companies and voluntary groups are all involved in providing old people's homes, sheltered housing schemes, aids to help old people and special housing for the elderly.

Lothian Homes Ltd.
PRIVATE
RETIREMENT
HOUSING
FOR SALE

Special features within these superb developments include:

MANAGEMENT SERVICE * EMERGENCY ALARM *
* LIFT * GUEST SUITE * GOLD MEDALLION
WHITE METER HEATING * ENTRYPHONE SYSTEM *
* DOUBLE GLAZING * WHEELCHAIR ACCESS *
* LANDSCAPED GROUNDS * CAR PARKING *

Planning for retirement

KIRSTI LITTLE reports on purpose built homes for the elderly that offer independence and all mod cons.

...In the past, when society's senior citizens were taken in and supported by the extended family network, it was less important to plan for retirement. Today, with social trends indicating rising numbers of pensioners, and more people owning homes and controlling their own destinies, many of us are actively planning a comfortable and rewarding old age...

Adequate provision for housing is perhaps one of the most important aspects of ensuring comfort and security for the elderly of the future, and to that end recent years have seen the emergence of a specialist sector of the property scene that has focussed attention on the retirement market...

Security and social interaction are two of the main reasons why many older buyers are choosing purpose-built retirement homes. "People of the same age group tend to enjoy similar hobbies and pastimes," says Beverley Brown of Slater Hogg & Howison. "They look out for each other's interests, and combine independence with a watchful eye."

The increasing number of people buying retirement homes has led to some building societies offering specialised lending facilities. As an alternative to the ordinary repayment mortgage, the Halifax Building Society offer a low-cost loan that keeps payments to a manageable minimum...

(source: *The Scotsman Magazine*, March 1988.)

WHAT IS SHELTERED HOUSING?

Retirement should mean living in comfort and security. For most people, the ideal in retirement is to remain independent in one's own home. Unfortunately, this is not always possible and for many the family house becomes too expensive or physically difficult to maintain, especially if there is also a large garden. Elderly people also encounter other difficulties such as too many stairs, inadequate heating, social isolation or may even live in remote locations. Moreover, help is not always readily available in times of accident or illness...

Sheltered housing was conceived, and exists to meet and help overcome these problems. Such housing is provided in groups of flats or cottages (normally 25 to 30) with a two-way speech alarm system linking each house with the warden's office and house. Many schemes also include a communal lounge, guest rooms and a laundry.

Occupiers of sheltered housing continue to be independent householders with all the rights and security which that entails...

Those who require social support in the form of Home Helps, Meals on Wheels, Community Nursing, etc. receive these services in the same way as other householders. The resident Warden offers the additional reassurance of a "good neighbour" who is available at regular times during the day and through the emergency alarm system, is always there overnight. Sheltered housing is, in short, a setting in which elderly persons may enjoy privacy combined with security, comfort and the knowledge that help or advice will be available if and when it is required.

(source: *Housing Association Information Pack*, Bield Housing Association Ltd)

When You're in Trouble and Alone

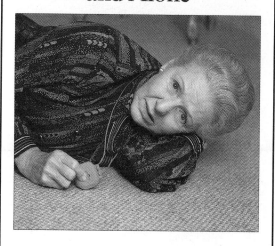

AID-CALL PLC
EMERGENCY MEDICAL ALARMS

QUESTIONS

1. Study the source extract on 'What is Sheltered Housing?'

   a) List five problems which many old people find in living in their own homes.

   b) Explain what sheltered housing is. Describe the features which help overcome the problems listed in your answer to (a).

2. What features, specially designed for old people, are highlighted in the advertisement for private retirement housing?

3. What problem facing old people does the advertisement for Aid-Call try to deal with?

4. Study the source extract on 'Planning for retirement'.

   a) Why does the article say it is more important today to plan for retirement?

   b) What two reasons are given for many old people buying 'purpose-built retirement homes'?

   c) How do some building societies help older people to buy their homes?

CASE STUDY

This case study about looking after elderly people illustrates some of the issues involved in the debate about how best to care for those in need.

'TAKING CARE OF GRANDAD'

The Jamieson family live in a three-bedroom, semi-detached bungalow in a new housing scheme on the outskirts of a large town. Tom Dickinson, Mrs Jamieson's father, lives on his own in an old flat in the centre of town. Mrs Dickinson died two years ago and Tom has managed to look after himself until recently but he suffers from arthritis and his health visitor has become concerned that he soon will find it difficult to cope alone.

Mary Jamieson - aged 42. She is Tom's daughter and only close relation living in Scotland. Her brother now lives in the south-east of England. Mary visits her father as often as she can since her mother's death, but her job as a secretary in a local lawyer's office means that this can only be at weekends or in the evening. She is finding the need to visit a strain and would like her father to come and live with the family.

Peter Jamieson - aged 44. Peter runs his own plumbing business and is beginning to feel that after several years of struggling to get the business established, he is now in a position to spend more time with his wife and family. He likes his father-in-law but is concerned about the strain his wife is under in caring for him. He is worried about the effects on the family if Tom comes to live with them. Peter would much rather that Tom went to live in an old people's home where he feels he would get more specialist care. He feels that if Tom's flat were sold, the family could afford to pay for a room in a private retirement home.

Tom Dickinson - aged 70. Tom likes his flat. He has lived in the area for almost thirty years. The flat has many memories of his wife. Tom knows, however, that as his arthritis has got worse, he has found the stairs to his flat more difficult, and he can't seem to keep the flat as clean and tidy as he would like. He also finds the old flat very cold in winter and he worries about his heating bills. He hates the thought of going to a home and would like to live with his daughter instead. One of his friends lives in a special sheltered housing scheme but Tom thinks that there is a long waiting list for these houses.

Janet Jamieson - aged 11. Janet has just started secondary school. Janet gets on very well with her Grandad and often accompanies her Mum in visiting him. She loves to go to see him on holidays, to run errands for him and to help around the flat. She likes to sit and listen to her Grandad telling stories about the past and about her Gran.

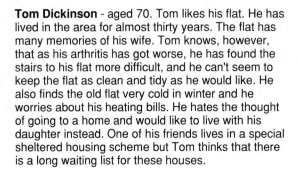

Colin Jamieson - aged 14. Colin has just started third year at school. He is a bright lad who enjoys school and does a lot of studying. He likes to bring his friends to his house and they spend their time talking and playing records in his room. He likes his Grandad and does not mind seeing him at Christmas and holidays but hates having to visit every weekend. He finds this boring and would much rather spend the time with his friends. He is very much against the idea of having to share his room with his younger sister.

A CTIVITIES

Study the information given in the case study and the resource material on housing for the elderly.

Split into groups of five. Each person in the group takes the part of one of the characters outlined above.

Imagine the family visits Grandad one weekend and Mrs Jamieson mentions again that Tom should think about giving up the flat and coming to live with them.

a) Act out the discussion that might follow.

b) What decision does your group reach about the best solution to the problem?

c) How does this compare with the other groups?

d) Make a list of all the issues involved in this family problem.

Put this list under the heading of 'personal', 'social' and 'economic' issues.

The Health Service

Another area where State services, private services and voluntary groups are involved in caring for us is that of health.

The basis of health care in the UK today is the National Health Service which was set up in 1948 to provide free health care for everyone.

The services which form the National Health Service are:

Dentists

Hospitals

Ambulance service

CHEMIST

Pharmacists

THE NATIONAL HEALTH SERVICE

District nurses

School Medical Service

Opticians

General practitioners

Health visitors
Midwives

Most of the money needed to run the National Health Service comes from taxation. In return many of the services provided are free – attending your doctor, treatment and stay in hospital, health services in school and so on. For some services such as dental treatment and medical prescriptions you have to pay part of the cost. However, a large number of people do not have to pay these charges – young people under 16, old age pensioners, pregnant women or those with children under one year old, and people on low incomes.

The National Health Service therefore provides a health service which is free or partly free for all citizens of the United Kingdom whether they are rich or poor. All services are linked, so that your local GP, your local hospital and your school medical services can all work together for your benefit. The Health Service also works to help prevent illness and tests people at school and at work to try to catch illnesses at a very early stage. It also works to explain to people the importance of fitness, healthy eating, not smoking and so on in order to have a healthy life.

Most people think the National Health Service has been an important development in improving British life, and generally we are much healthier now than we were when the National Health Service was set up. The Health Service does have serious problems, however. There are long hospital waiting lists, especially for non-emergency operations. Hospitals are sometimes short of equipment such as dialysis machines to treat people with kidney failure. Hospitals are sometimes old and in need of modernisation. There are sometimes shortages of nurses and other staff.

Patients who have to live with pain

A 60-year-old woman hobbles with a stick into the consulting room at St Charles Hospital in west London. An X-ray of her hips has just been placed before Nigel Harris, the orthopaedic surgeon. "Dreadful, quite dreadful," he told her. "You need both those done."

The woman is exceptionally stoical and uncomplaining. It takes patient questioning to extract from her that she cares for her 70-year-old invalid husband, who cannot go out; her daughter has to do any heavy shopping; she cannot raise her legs high enough to climb on a bus; she dare not sit in a chair for too long, because it becomes so difficult to get up and the pain in her left hip keeps her awake at night.

This is not the life and death side of the National Health Service, but these are patients suffering considerable pain.

Mr Harris's clinic is loaded with patients from all over the country – a woman from Brighton with trapped wrist nerves, which makes her hands acutely painful and almost useless; a sheet metal worker from Shropshire with a bent finger which stops him working; a man from Surrey with hip trouble.

All are there because their GPs told them the wait locally just for an out-patient appointment – let alone an operation – was between six and 15 months.

(source: *Cash, Crisis and Cure: The Independent Guide to the NHS Debate* by Nicholas Timmins.)

Demand for beds that cannot be met

The elderly neighbour of a 75-year-old man had spent an hour in a draughty passage waiting for a telephone call from St Bartholomew's Hospital, London, to find out if a bed was free. After 17 months on the waiting-list the old man's appointment for a knee replacement had arrived. But Bart's on Monday was short of seven orthopaedic beds.

A 76-year-old woman waiting for a hip replacement had her appointment postponed. A friend had taken time off work to bring her in. "The problem is we don't have a bed spare," Lesley Scott, the hospital bed manager, explained. Her daily task is to squeeze a quart into a pint pot as Bart's struggles with its own closed beds against more than 900 beds closed this year in inner London.

(source: *Cash, Crisis and Cure: The Independent Guide to the NHS Debate* by Nicholas Timmins.)

Many different explanations have been given for these problems and the debate we have seen on the future of the Welfare State applies equally to the future of the National Health Service.

There are people who think that the National Health Service is a victim of its own success. More and more people are being kept alive longer and there are many old people in need of medical care. The NHS is now able to treat and cure illnesses in ways that would have seemed like miracles when the NHS was set up.

However, some of the newer treatments, such as heart surgery, are very expensive. According to this viewpoint the NHS requires more money to be spent on it in order for it to continue to be successful.

On the other hand there are people who agree that the National Health Service has done a magnificent job but who feel that it has grown too big, that it does not offer people any choice of treatment and that those who can afford to pay for medical treatment should do so, leaving the National Health Service to care for those who cannot pay.

People who wish to receive private health care can pay for this through private health insurance and in recent years this type of insurance has become more popular.

Numbers covered by private health insurance

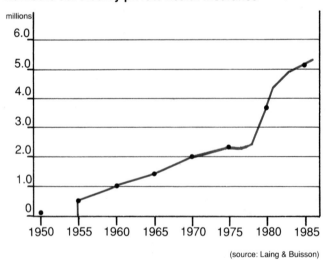

(source: Laing & Buisson)

BUPACare

Britain feels better for it.

WHAT BUPA CAN MEAN TO YOU

Today three million people in Britain belong to BUPA.

Like you and your family they want the assurance that in the event of serious illness or injury they can afford the benefits of private medical treatment.

They have joined for the great difference that BUPA makes when you are ill. Like having a say in where and when you are treated, and even by whom.

Our members give many individual reasons for joining. Here are some of them.

"First and foremost, I want to be able to go into hospital without delay."
With BUPA, you'll have the advantage of being treated promptly for any problem that you are unexpectedly faced with. And you'll be able to choose a time to go into hospital that suits you, to fit in with your work, your home life or your holiday plans.

"It's important to pick the right person for the job."
Going privately means that, with your doctor's help, you can choose the most appropriate specialist to treat you.

"I'd like to go into a modern hospital."
With your specialist's help you will be able to choose the hospital which suits you best. One which provides the medical facilities you need to get better and, if you feel it's important, a hospital close to your home.

"I need privacy, peace and quiet."
Rest and a good night's sleep are not always possible in large busy wards, but in a private room you will have the peace and quiet you need when you are ill.

Most private rooms have their own bathroom, radio, colour TV and telephone facilities to make you feel more comfortable and more at home, and a "nurse call" system to keep you in constant touch with the nursing team.

"I wanted my family and friends to be able to visit at the times they found easiest."
Staying in a private room means your visitors will be able to call in at almost any time. They're not restricted by hospital routine to times which may be inconvenient – for instance, for a busy husband trying to look after the family. Within reason, visitors will be able to stay as long as they *and you* like.

(source: BUPA leaflet)

What it costs

...Paying can have advantages: a guarantee of who will carry out the operation and, most importantly, where and when it will be done. On the NHS you are referred to a consultant by your GP. If your case is not urgent you have to wait for a bed and the consultant cannot guarantee whether it will be him or one of his team who will carry out the operation...

The real advantage of private care for British patients is for non-urgent operations which are constantly pushed down and off the Health Service lists. 'Private care provides the certainty that you will get a bed at the time you want it. That is a number one problem with the Health Service,' said surgeon Averil Mansfield. 'The uncertainty of whether a patient who has been sent for will actually get a bed when they arrive at the hospital is bad for us and much worse for the patient. If you're working, it's terrible – you cancel all your appointments, go into hospital, and someone says, "Sorry mate, no bed, go home again."'...

Many of the simplest operations done in private hospitals are now carried out in day centres, where costs for minor procedures are set out in a menu form. At the Princess Grace Hospital in London, for example, you can have a wart removed for £150, a skin graft for £295, or a nerve tendon repaired for £375.

The cost of a private operation varies from patient to patient. For most, there isn't one bill at the end of the day, but three – one from the surgeon, another from the anaesthetist and a third from the hospital, which charges for everything from your bed (between £150 and £300 a night), to the surgeon's gloves (£5.58), to two Paracetamol tablets (14p).
(Ann Morris)

(source: *The Observer Magazine*, 17 July 1988)

The state of the Health Service

...The policy of the present Conservative government... has been to try to restrict increased spending on the NHS and encourage the further development of private sector health care.

To supporters of this policy, private practice will act as a 'safety valve' for an overworked NHS. However, it is important to realise that what private health is willing and able to achieve in this direction is strictly limited.

Very few people are rich enough to be sure of being able to pay for the medical treatment they might need. Most people wanting private health care are, therefore, dependent on a health insurance scheme. The problem here is that insurance schemes are restricted. They frequently do not cover, for example, long term care of the elderly or chronically sick...

The result of this is that those groups in society who tend to be in most need of health care, such as the elderly, mentally ill, chronically sick, the low paid and the unemployed are still going to be dependent on state health care. The experience of countries such as the United States, where private health insurance schemes flourish, suggests that such a health policy tends to produce a rigid 'two-tier' system of health care, where the affluent and insured monopolise the best health care facilities and medical personnel at the expense of the rest of the population.
(source: S Taylor and L Jordan, *Health and Illness*, Longman 1986.)

1. What are the main principles which lie behind the National Health Service?

2. In what ways have you been affected by the National Health Service since your birth?

3. What success has the National Health Service had?

4. What problems is the National Health Service experiencing?

5. Read the source extract, 'What BUPA Can Mean to You'.

   a) List the benefits which the extract claims for private health treatment.

   b) Do you think the National Health Service can provide this type of benefit? Give reasons for your answer.

6. Read the source extracts, 'What it Costs' and 'The State of the Health Service'.

   a) What is the main advantage of private health care?

   b) In what ways does private health care in hospital lead to three bills?

   c) What groups of people tend *not* to be covered by private health insurance?

   d) In what ways can private medicine produce a 'two-tier' system of health care?

7. Here is an extract taken from one of the major political parties' manifestoes. Identify which political party produced this statement.

"We welcome the growth in private health insurance in recent years. This has both made more health care available, and lightened the load on the NHS. . . . . We shall continue to encourage this valuable supplement to state care."

Divide into four groups. Each group should take one of the statements below. Each group member should then write down arguments for and against their statement. Choose someone in your group to act as chairperson and discuss the arguments for and against the statement.

a) 'It is not fair that those who can afford to pay privately should be able to jump the queue to get immediate medical treatment.'

b) 'People who can afford it should contribute to the National Health Service by paying for visits to the doctor and for their stay in hospital.'

c) 'People who choose private health care should not have to pay taxes towards the National Health Service.'

d) 'The Government should increase taxation so that more money would be available for spending on the National Health Service.'

Poverty

There are about 56 million people in the United Kingdom. Many people – perhaps as many as 18 million – live in poverty. This means that their income and living standards are low. There are various reasons for people living in poverty:

- They are unemployed and are unable to find work.
- They are sick or disabled so they cannot work.
- They are in work but earn a low wage.
- They cannot work full-time because they are looking after children (this applies particularly to single-parent families) or old people.
- They are too old to work.

Many people are born into poor families and grow up to be poor themselves. This is known as the **cycle of poverty** and can be very difficult to break out of.

THE CYCLE OF POVERTY

FAMILY LIFE
Poverty causes family problems – depression, family quarrels and broken marriages. One-parent families common. Children born into families with poor opportunities.

EDUCATION
Children have poor education. Parents had poor education and do not encourage children. Often local schools have high truancy rate. Children leave school with few qualifications.

HOUSING
Likely to stay in poor housing. Areas likely to have high crime rates and social problems. Lack of amenities such as parks, leisure centres.

EMPLOYMENT
Lack of employment opportunities. Likely to do low-paid work. Higher chance of unemployment.

SOCIAL SECURITY

The Welfare State provides a variety of **benefits** for those in need which are designed to give a regular income that people can live on.

– For unemployed people the Welfare State provides unemployment benefit. For the long-term unemployed there is a benefit called Income Support.

– For sick and disabled people the Welfare State provides sickness benefit, invalidity benefits and disablement benefits.

– For low wage-earners the Welfare State provides Family Credit.

– For families bring up children the Welfare State provides Child Benefit and single-parent families there is a One-Parent benefit.

– For old-age pensioners the Welfare State provides the Retirement Pension.

As with other aspects of the Welfare State there are differing views on how best to help poor people.

A Some people argue that the State should increase the level of benefits provided to help poor people to break out of their cycle of poverty. They believe that:

• Emphasis should be placed on creating 'real jobs' rather than 'creating' jobs through Government training schemes.
• The State should insist upon employers paying a **minimum wage** to solve the problem of the poverty trap, because people can receive more in benefits than they can earn in working for low wages.
• High wage earners should pay more in taxes to provide a better level of benefits for those in need.

B Other people argue that when the State hands out benefits it discourages people from looking after themselves and actually prevents people from breaking out of the cycle of poverty. They say that:

• Rather than increase all State benefits, benefits should be directed towards the really needy through means-testing.
• Efforts should be made to discourage and penalise people who claim benefits to which they are not entitled.
• People should be encouraged to look for work and be re-trained for work in new growth industries.
• Setting national minimum wages only puts up employers' costs and discourages employers from taking on new workers.
• High taxation should be lowered to encourage people to work harder and to encourage employers to expand, thus creating more work.

These two extracts from policy documents from the Conservative and Labour Parties illustrate the two different approaches to solving the problems of unemployment and poverty.

PEOPLE AT WORK
LABOUR OBJECTIVES

...It is against this backcloth of new opportunities and challenges, and of major changes in employment, that we set out Labour's central objectives for people at work. First, we aim to create an economy in which every individual has the chance to develop and use their talents and skills to the full. That is why our commitment to full employment lies at the very heart of our economic policy. That is why we are determined to develop a new strategy for education and training. For we know that Britain can only succeed if it has a work force that is highly trained and highly adaptable – one that is able to respond quickly to changing technologies and changing customer demands.

ECONOMIC EQUALITY

A civilised society provides for its vulnerable members so that they too may share in its resources and participate in its opportunities.

...By 1991 continuing unemployment, low wages and inadequate benefits will leave some 18 million adults and children – one in three of the population – living on or below the poverty level.

...This year's Budget gave more in tax cuts to the top one per cent of taxpayers than it gave to the seventy per cent who are on average and below-average incomes. In income tax cuts alone, these 250,000 richest taxpayers received the equivalent of the entire increase in the social security budget this April for over twelve million people claiming benefit.

...It is both offensive and undemocratic that the wealthy should celebrate tax cuts while the poor struggle with benefit cuts.

...First, we must create opportunities for the unemployed and others excluded from employment to find work. Second, we must deal with the problem of low pay. Third, we need a new system of social security, one which allows independence and ensures a decent standard of living for those who rely upon it.

...We want to see fewer people obliged to live on means-tested benefits. Unemployment is the single most important cause of poverty in Britain today. The overwhelming majority of people living on income support would like nothing better than to earn a decent living.

...After unemployment, the second major cause of poverty among people of working age is low pay. Wider opportunities for employment are not enough if we only open the door to jobs paying poverty-level wages.

...Labour believes in providing adequate wages in the first place rather than using means-tested benefits – such as family credit – to subsidise pay.

(source: *Social Justice and Economic Efficiency*, The Labour Party.)

'The Next Moves Forward'
CONSERVATIVE OBJECTIVES
LOWER TAXES

We are the only Party that believes in lower taxation.

As the Party determined to achieve growing prosperity we recognise that it is people who create wealth, not governments. Lower taxation coupled with lower inflation makes everyone better off. It encourages people to work harder, to be inventive and to take risks. It promotes a climate of enterprise and initiative.

High taxes deprive people of their independence and make their choices for them. The desire to do better for one's family is one of the strongest motives in human nature. As a Party committed to the family and opposed to the over-powerful State, we want people to keep more of what they earn, and to have more freedom of choice about what they do for themselves, their families and for others less fortunate.

HELPING UNEMPLOYED PEOPLE INTO JOBS

As well as creating a climate in which business could employ more people, we have developed programmes to help those out of work.

The *Youth Training Scheme (YTS)* caters for all school-leavers aged 16 and 17 who wish to participate in training and work experience. Every trainee is given the opportunity of working towards a recognised qualification.

The new *Job Training Scheme (JTS)*, which started in April this year, will offer a chance to any person over 18 who has been unemployed for six months or more, who wants to work and train with an employer for a recognised qualification. This year it will help over 26,000 people in Scotland.

Under our *Community Programme*, each year over 30,000 Scots who have been out of work for some time gain valuable experience working on community projects.

Under the *Enterprise Allowance Scheme* this year, 7,000 people who have been unemployed for some time will start to work for themselves in Scotland. Nearly 20,000 have benefited so far. Many of them have become employers themselves.

Job Clubs were first opened in 1985 to help the unemployed help themselves back into jobs. 110 have now been established in Scotland. At present two thirds of those leaving Job Clubs go into employment – in Scotland that means over 3,000 people.

Although youth unemployment has declined in the last year it still remains a problem. Far too many of our youngsters leave school with an education that has failed to prepare them for the world of work. At the same time, by maintaining high starting wages comparable to those of fully trained craftsmen, trade unions have kept many of them out of work.

In 1983 we introduced the first Youth Training Scheme. It is now a national two-year programme aimed at giving young people qualifications for work.

The First Guarantee

We will now guarantee a place on the Youth Training Scheme to every school-leaver under 18 who is not going directly into a job. As a result, none of these school-leavers need be unemployed. They can remain at school, move to college, get a job, or receive a guaranteed training. YTS will serve as a bridge between school and work.

We will take steps to ensure that those under 18 who deliberately choose to remain unemployed are not eligible for benefit.

SOCIAL SECURITY - A FAIR DEAL FOR THOSE IN NEED

We are spending £46 billion this year on social security benefits – over £800 a year for every man, woman and child in the country. Expenditure on pensions and other benefits has risen by £13 billion on top of inflation since we came into office. Most of this – an extra £9 billion – has gone to provide better standards of help and support to more elderly people, families with children, disabled people and those suffering long-term illness. The other 4 billion has gone to help the unemployed.

For the first time for 40 years the Government has undertaken an overall review of the social security system. The review showed a social security system which was too complex and which too often did not provide help for those most in need. The 1986 Social Security Act tackled these problems and reformed the position so that the system is simpler to understand and to run. It will be fairer in the way it directs help to those who need it most. And will be a system in which people can look forward to independence and security in retirement.
(source: *The Next Moves Forward*, Conservative Party Central Office.)

QUESTIONS

1. List five reasons why people may be, or become, poor.

2. Explain in your own words what the 'cycle of poverty' is.

3. Name the benefits which the Welfare State provides for the following:
   a) elderly people;
   b) unemployed people;
   c) low wage-earners;
   d) families with children;
   e) disabled people.

4. What are the arguments for and against:
   a) 'means-tested' benefits;
   b) high taxation for the wealthy;
   c) a minimum national wage.

5. Using the Conservative extract, answer the following:
   a) What is the Conservative Party policy on taxation?
   b) What reasons are given in favour of this policy?
   c) List the various programmes which the Conservative Government has introduced to help those out of work.

   d) What two reasons does the Conservative Party give for high levels of youth unemployment?
   e) What is the Youth Training Scheme?
   f) What justification does the Conservative Party give for not giving benefits to young people under 18?
   g) What groups of people does the Conservative Party claim to have helped through their spending on social security?
   h) What criticisms of the social security system does the Conservative Party claim its review showed?
   i) In what ways does the Conservative Party claim to have solved these problems?

6. Using the Labour Party extract answer the following:
   a) What are the Labour Party's aims for people at work?
   b) 'A civilised society provides for its vulnerable members.' To which 'vulnerable members' is the Labour Party referring?
   c) What reasons does the Labour Party give for its view that in 1991, 'one in three of the population' will be in poverty?
   d) Why does the Labour Party criticise the 1988 Budget (referred to as 'this year's Budget')?
   e) What three aims does the Labour Party set out for dealing with poverty?
   f) Does the Labour Party agree or disagree with means-tested benefits? Find a sentence in the extract to support your answer.
   g) What is the Labour Party policy on low pay? Find a sentence in the extract to support your answer.

ACTIVITY

Make use of the section above and the two source extracts to write down your views on the following statements. You may also want to read the section on unemployment in Unit 2, 'Who Do You Depend On?'

– Means-tested benefits require investigation into people's circumstances. This can make people feel inadequate and failures in society. As a result means-testing can discourage people from claiming benefits.

– Too many and too high a level of State benefit discourages people from taking responsibility for themselves.

– Young people who leave school at 16 and refuse to go into training should not receive State benefits.

– Taking high taxes from wealthy people discourages them from working hard and helps to create unemployment.

– A national minimum wage is the only way to stop the problem of low wages.

– Social Security 'scroungers' are ruining the Welfare State.

Charities and voluntary help

Help the Aged

Shelter SCOTTISH CAMPAIGN FOR THE HOMELESS

The Samaritans

Save the Children

People in need have for many years been helped by charities. In earlier times the churches provided most of the help, collecting money to give out to poor people, and providing food and clothing. During the nineteenth century a number of well-known charities were formed. In 1870 Thomas Barnado founded his first orphanage. The Salvation Army was also set up in the second part of the nineteenth century to help destitute and homeless people in London.

These charities were set up before the Welfare State was established. However, the growth of the Welfare State has not lessened the need for work of charities and volunteers. Rather, the work of these groups has increased. What part do charities play in our welfare society?

• They plug gaps in the help provided by the Welfare State. For example, drug addicts, alcoholics and down-and-outs receive more direct help from groups such as Salvation Army and Alcoholics Anonymous than from the Government.

• They act as pressure groups to put pressure on the Government to provide more help. Shelter and the Child Poverty Action Group are two examples of charities who act forcefully as pressure groups.

• They provide ordinary people with an opportunity to volunteer to work with people in need. Many young people spend some of their spare time working with such groups. Community Service Volunteers provides a variety of voluntary community work for people. Many schools and youth clubs organise community service for their students.

• They help people in need to help themselves. People who join Alcoholics Anonymous provide help and support for each other.

A CTIVITIES

1. Here is a list of voluntary groups. Choose one of them and try to find out more about the type of work which it does. You can use your local library or find their address in the telephone book and write to them for information.

Shelter   Salvation Army   Imperial Cancer Research Child Poverty Action Group   Save the Children Red Cross   Samaritans   Age Concern

2. Try to find out the names and activities of other caring voluntary organisations.

3. Divide into groups of four. Choose one of these two statements. Use five minutes to write down your views. Choose a group chairperson and discuss the arguments for and against the statement.

– If the Welfare State was doing its job properly there would be no need for charities and voluntary work.

– It is wrong that charities should have to depend upon flag days and other forms of fund-raising.

– The Government should have a form of charity tax which would be deducted from people's wages, to be given to the charities. The amount each organisation received would depend on the scope of

KEYWORDS

The following Keywords are used in this Unit. Make sure you have understood what they mean.

welfare society	**welfare 'safety net'**
Welfare State	**means-tested benefits**
right	**National Health Service**
principle	**private health insurance**
cycle of poverty	**national insurance**
sheltered housing	

2
CONTRASTS IN SOCIETY

CLASS IN SOCIETY

'From each according to his ability to each according to his needs' (Karl Marx).

We all share the need for food, clothing, shelter, education, good health and opportunities to enjoy ourselves. Yet a few moments' thought will tell us that people in different situations also need different things. A baby's needs are different from a teenager's (see Chapter 5).

'All men are created equal' (American Declaration of Independence). We are all human but it is obvious that some people have a far easier time satisfying their needs than others (see Chapter 5).

How important are these differences and what do they tell us about society today?

My £400,000 regret, by pools winner Kathy

By DAVID WICKHAM

GOSSIP has ruined life for pools winner Kathy Collett.

She said yesterday: "I wish we had never seen the money."

A year ago Peter Collett won £447,055 on Littlewoods Pools.

At the time he said the win wouldn't change the lives of him and Kathy, who serves meals at the local school.

He said they would probably move to a detached house and buy a new car. Neither of them planned to give up work.

But at their council house home in Rynal Street, Evesham, Worcestershire, Kathy said: "I wish we had never won the pools. Peter suffers from nerves and I'm almost frightened to go out.

"When I go shopping I can see people watching what I buy in the supermarket, so – just to let them know we are still working class – I put a jar of jam in my basket.

"We were happy before we won the pools, but the pressures on us have been enormous.

"Even now there are people on the estate who gossip about us because we haven't moved out of our council house. They think we should be living in a big flash house with all the trimmings.

"But we are working class people, we have always been working class, and we intend to stay that way.

"We are trying to live the life we want and we don't want the money to get in the way."

(source: *News on Sunday*, 8 November 1987.)

These three stories tell us that these families have different amounts of money to spend on necessities. They say something about different groups or **classes** in our society. However, money is not the only way of describing different groups in society.

1. Copy this table and write a sentence about each family.

POOR _____

WELL-OFF _____

RICH _____

2. In the extract on page 105, why does Kathy say, "I wish we had never seen the money"?

3. Why does Kathy say, "We have always been working class"?

4. Write down phrases from the passage which suggest that Kathy and Peter are working-class.

There seems more to 'class' than just money. People often use phrases like **working-class**, **middle-class** and **upper-class** when they are talking about class, and they often have strong opinions about which class they feel they belong to.

Self-rated Social Class, UK, 1986

| | Percentages and numbers | |
Social Class	Self	Parents
Upper middle	1	2
Middle	24	17
Upper working	21	12
Working	48	59
Poor	3	8
Don't know, no response	3	2
Sample size (= 100%) (numbers)	3066	3066

(source: Martin Slattery, *Official Statistics*, 1986.)

*A*CTIVITIES

1. Carry out a survey in your school using the classes in the table. This will give you some idea of the social structure of the area you live in. You may find that your answers are quite different from those in the table. This is because the people in your school come from quite a small area whereas the table covers the whole of the United Kingdom.

2. Interview some teachers in your school and ask them which class they belong to.

3. Discuss, either in small groups or as a class, whether it is money or a person's job or other factors which decide a person's social class. You should use the phrases 'working-class', 'middle-class' and 'upper-class' as the starting point of your discussion.

What is class?

Sociologists have found it very difficult to come up with a definition of social class which is clear to everybody.

Working-class: might suggest that if you work for a living then you are working-class. Nowadays just about everybody works or would like to work.

Middle-class: in terms of what people can afford to buy most people have things in their homes which even a few years ago would have been thought of as luxuries for the well-off. Yet most people do not call themselves middle-class.

Upper-class: this phrase tends to suggest great inherited wealth and often a title such as 'Lord' or 'Lady'. There are so few people who actually fit this description as to make it almost meaningless.

However, social class does have a profound effect on what are called our **life chances**.

It becomes important, then, to have some generally agreed method showing the differences between groups. This allows us to identify those groups which have greatest difficulty in meeting their needs. This is the job of the person who studies how people and society behave, the **sociologist**. As a society we then have to decide whether it is right or desirable to do things to improve the situation. This is the **politician's** job.

In your discussion about class you may have mentioned some of the following factors which decide a person's social class: income, job, education, power, speech, accent, dress, appearance, behaviour, habits, lifestyle.

Although many of these factors are very important, all except the first three (income, job and education) are very hard to measure. Most definitions of social class are based on a person's job because: a) your job determines your income; b) your income affects your life chances; c) your education and training affects your job.

Most of the other factors are influenced by the first three.

The most widely used method of defining social class is that used by the **Registrar General** who is the government official responsible for carrying out the **census of population** every ten years. The following table shows the way in which the population is grouped in the census.

I	Professional occupations
II	Intermediate occupations (including most managerial and senior administrative occupations)
IIIN	Skilled occupations (non-manual)
IIIM	Skilled occupations (manual)
IV	Partly skilled occupations
V	Unskilled occupations
Other	Residual groups including, for example, armed forces, students, and those whose occupation was inadequately described.

(source: *Social Trends* 1989. Reproduced with the kind permission of the Controller of HMSO.)

Sometimes these categories will be grouped together in different ways to form a smaller number of classes. Advertising agents use the letters A, B, C1, C2, D and E, but they mean roughly the same thing.

A CTIVITIES

1. Make up a diagram which shows the links between a person's job, education and income. Write in the other features of social class as well.

2. Choose a picture from a magazine or newspaper which tells you something about a person's job. Write a story about that person's 'life chances' using the information in the table below.

Social class is probably the most important influence on our lives:

● Birth – children of unskilled working-class parents are three times more likely to die within a year of birth than the children of professionals;
● Health – working-class people are three times more likely to have a serious illness than middle-class people. They are six times more likely to get arthritis and rheumatism;
● Family life – working-class people marry younger, have slightly larger families and are more likely to divorce than middle-class people;
● Housing – eighty-five per cent of the upper middle class own their own houses compared to 25 per cent of the unskilled working class;
● Income – the higher up the social class you climb the larger your income;
● Education – the middle classes are more successful in the education system and 60 per cent of the upper middle class have been to university or polytechnic;
● Politics – the higher your social class, the greater the chance you vote Conservative;
● Death – a man with a professional job can expect to live seven years longer on average than a man with a labouring job.

(source: S. Moore, *Sociology Alive*, Stanley Thornes.)

3. Write a list of as many jobs as you can and sort them out into groups according to the Registrar General's groups.

Here is a range of information which points out the differences between groups in our society.

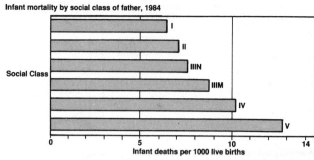

Infant mortality by social class of father, 1984

(source: Office of Population Censuses and Surveys, 1984.)

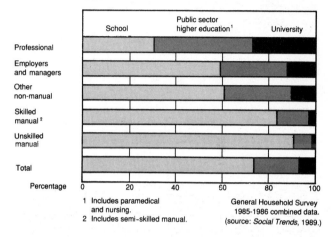

EDUCATION

1 Includes paramedical and nursing.
2 Includes semi-skilled manual.

General Household Survey 1985-1986 combined data.
(source: *Social Trends*, 1989.)

Background factors thought very important to a successful marriage		
	Adequate income	Good housing
Social Class:		
I/II	27%	22%
III Non-manual	29%	29%
III Manual	42%	40%
IV/V	40%	42%

(source: *British Social Attitudes*. The 1987 Report.)

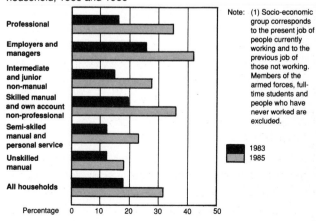

Video-recorder ownership by head of household, 1983 and 1985

Note: (1) Socio-economic group corresponds to the present job of people currently working and to the previous job of those not working. Members of the armed forces, full-time students and people who have never worked are excluded.

1983
1985

(source: General Household Survey, 1983 and 1985.)

HOUSING

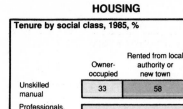

Tenure by social class, 1985, %

	Owner-occupied	Rented from local authority or new town	Private rental
Unskilled manual	33	58	9
Professionals, employers and managers	86	4	10

SMOKING

Cigarette smoking by social class, 1984

% 0 10 20 30 40 50

Male — Professional / Unskilled manual

Female

HOLIDAYS

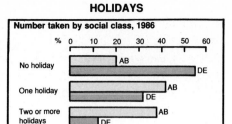

Number taken by social class, 1986

% 0 10 20 30 40 50 60

No holiday — AB / DE

One holiday — AB / DE

Two or more holidays — AB / DE

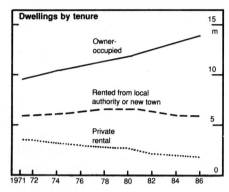

Dwellings by tenure

Owner-occupied

Rented from local authority or new town

Private rental

1971 72 74 76 78 80 82 84 86

15 m 10 5 0

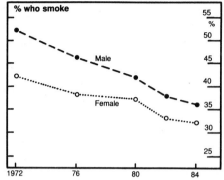

% who smoke

Male

Female

1972 76 80 84

55 % 50 45 40 35 30 25

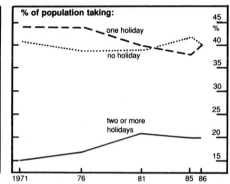

% of population taking:

one holiday

no holiday

two or more holidays

1971 76 81 85 86

45 % 40 35 30 25 20 15

ILLNESS

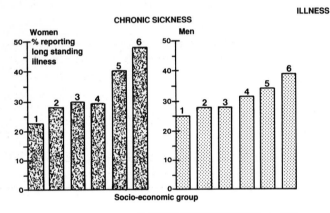

CHRONIC SICKNESS

Women — % reporting long standing illness

1 2 3 4 5 6

Men

1 2 3 4 5 6

Socio-economic group

ACUTE SICKNESS

Women — % reporting acute illness

1 2 3 4 5 6

Men

1 2 3 4 5 6

Socio-economic group

(source: OPCS (1986) General Household Survey, 1984.)

Death-rates for 16-64-year-old age groups

Socio-economic group	1921-3	1930-2	1949-53	1959-63	1970-2
Professional	82	90	86	76	77
Managerial and lower professional	94	94	92	81	81
Skilled manual	95	97	101	100	104
Semi-skilled manual	101	102	104	103	113
Unskilled manual	125	111	118	143	137

(source: *Social Trends, 1985* Reproduced with the permission of the Controller of HMSO.)

Voting by class

Percentages. (Figures in brackets show change since '83.)

Class:	CON	LAB	LSD	OTHER
AB (Prof/managerial)	54 (-1)	13 (-2)	30 (+3)	3 (0)
C1 (Clerical)	47 (-2)	24 (+4)	26 (-3)	2 (0)
C2 (Skilled manual)	42 (+4)	35 (+3)	21 (-5)	2 (-2)
DE (Semi/unskilled manual)	31 (+1)	46 (+1)	20 (-2)	3 (0)

(source: *The Independent*, 13 June 1987.)

A CTIVITIES

1. For each of the graphs or tables write a sentence which describes the differences between social groups. Remember to mention any trends that appear through time.

2. Working as a group, you could try to find more information from other sources about these differences.

Although social class is a very important factor in determining life chances it is not the only one. Whether you are a man or a woman, black or white, young or old, in work or unemployed, the part of the country you live in may be equally important in affecting your opportunities.

Perhaps none of these things really matters? People who manage to fit into the system may survive reasonably well. Yet some observers have suggested that a new class is emerging – an **underclass** with little or no place in society.

Out but not down in smile city

ON prime-time television tonight... an articulate victim's commentary will jolt the comfortable lives of many viewers who would prefer not to see dispatches from their own underclass... "the way the system's geared, once you're down you can't get up. This society is a me society. You just can't move because everyone's saying: 'Out of my way, it's me first!' If you are at the bottom of the heap you are trodden on, you are stood on...

"The city fathers sit there in their infinite folly, thinking, 'It's a wonderful wee place' because they issue wee daft badges with a smile on. But they forget that if you turn that upside down, it tells you how people really are."

(source: *The Scotsman*, 7 November 1988.)

Q UESTIONS

1. In the newspaper article the person says, "This society is a me society. You just can't move. . ." Do you agree that people at 'the bottom of the heap' are stuck? Give a reason for your answer.

2. Explain how people might change from one social class to another.

A CTIVITIES

1. Make a collection of pictures and headlines about the 'life chances' of one or more of the social classes: underclass, working class, middle class, upper class. Look for these features: babies, food, holidays, jobs, pets, houses, cars, clothes, sports, smokers, health, black women and men, older and younger people, different regions.

Make a display from your collection. You can take ideas about the differences from other parts of this chapter. Your display could compare one class with another.

2. Write a script and present your display to your group or class.

3. You or your whole class could present a report on social class and other differences.

KEYWORDS

The following Keywords are used in this Unit. Make sure you have understood what they mean.

needs
classes
working-class
middle-class
upper-class
social structure
life chances
sociologist
politician
Registrar General
census of population
underclass

THE HAVES AND THE HAVE-NOTS

In Britain there are many different levels of wealth and **standards of living**. Some people earn high salaries, can afford costly houses and are able to lead expensive **lifestyles**. Even with higher tax rates than poorer people, many of the wealthy still have 'loadsamoney'.

Other people are the '**have-nots**', who do not have a high standard of living, are often in **poverty**, and do not have the freedom and choices of the wealthy. In the following pages we shall look at some of these differences in society in Britain.

Contrasts in earnings

Some people have more money to spend on their way of life because they earn much more than other people.

High earners

A CITY banker earning £2.5 million a year – over £48,000 a week or £6,883 every day – has emerged as Britain's highest-paid businessman...

This puts him in a pay bracket of his own for businessmen and enough to rival the incomes of rock stars, film actors, and members of royalty.

Less fashionable industry and commerce are lagging far behind the City in terms of pay, with only the Burton Group chairman, Sir Ralph Halpern, rated at more than £1 million a year. The chairman of ICI makes £393,000.
(source: *Guardian Weekly*, 18 October 1987.)

LOW EARNERS

Four out of five part-time jobs are done by women either because that's all they can get, or because they have to fit the hours around child-care.

Delores works part-time at a private nursing home in Manchester for £1.72 an hour.

"For a nurse the pay is rotten, but being part-time means I can look after my kids, which is the most important thing," says Delores, 31, who is usually the only nurse on night duty looking after a home full of frail old folks.

Jobs like nursing, cleaning, catering and shop assistants are filled largely by part-timers.

And because these jobs are often treated as low status by society and employers, they are usually low paid with poor terms and conditions of employment....
(source: *News on Sunday*, 13 September 1987.)

WEEKLY EARNINGS (1987)

Farm Worker — £120
Policewoman — ?
T.V. personality — £1200
High Court Judge — £150
Nurse — ?
£260
£7000

QUESTIONS

1. Apart from the city banker, what other groups are mentioned as having high earnings?
2. Which two companies pay their chairman high wages?
3. What kind of jobs are often done by part-timers?
4. Why is it mainly women who do these part-time jobs?
5. Why are these jobs often low paid?

110

1. In groups of four or five, study the earnings diagram on p.110, and discuss the items included.

2. List the weekly earnings in a 'league table', beginning with the highest.

3. Beside each item of earnings, put the job you think matches it.

4. Check your two lists with the other groups' lists to see how they compare.

5. Why do you think a TV personality is paid much more than a nurse?

6. Do you think this is fair to the nurse, considering her or his valuable work in society?

7. For what reasons are each of the following highly paid: a) a Surgeon; b) a High Court Judge; c) a Chief Fire Officer?

8. Apart from earning money by working, what other types of income might people have?

Different lifestyles

For most people, their **lifestyle** –the way they live – is decided by how much income they have. All individuals, families, and countries try to have a **budget** – a balance between income and spending.

As we have seen, people have widely differing levels of earning and income. These inequalities in income can lead to widely differing lifestyles. For example, if the lifestyle of the Prince and Princess of Wales is compared with the lifestyle of an average young married couple, many differences show up.

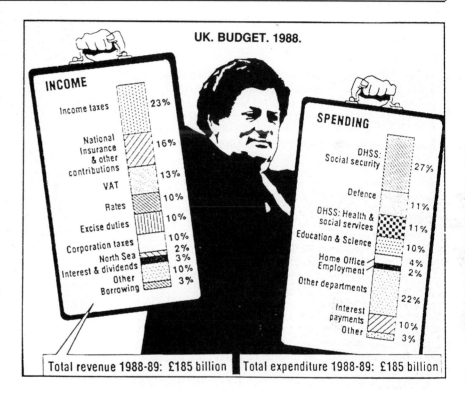

. . . HOW THE COUPLES LIVE . . .

	HOMES	INCOME	CARS	HOLIDAYS	CLOTHES	FUN
CHARLES & DIANA	Highgrove, a £1 million stately home. Plus use of all Royal palaces	£1 million a year as Duke of Cornwall. Plus several millions from investments	An Aston Martin, a Jaguar, three Fords and a Range Rover	Caribbean, Italy, Lichtenstein and Scotland. Plus numerous official trips	They both buy from top designers. Diana reputedly spent £100,000 for her Italian tour	For Charles, it's polo, the opera and walking. For Di, pop music and dancing
SIMON & SUSAN	A modest little semi-detached house in Leeds bought with a mortgage for £18,000	Less than £200 a week earned from his little baker's shop in Leeds	A company-owned Ford Cortina Estate, provided by his father's bakery business	One week a year at a caravan site in Filey, North Yorks. Never been abroad	They spend only £20 a month in stores like Marks and Spencer's	About four times a year they pop out for a pizza– and they watch lots of TV

(source: *News of the World*, 21 July 1985.)

Since people's lifestyles are linked to their income, any change which affects that income can affect the lifestyle. In cases where people's income is reduced, serious hardships may be caused, particularly if people cannot balance their budget and they fall into debt.

Lifestyles may also change over a period of years. The information below, from a Government publication, *Britain 1989*, indicates some changes in lifestyle of the average British citizen.

debt trap

IT WASN'T raining, but a stiff, damp November breeze blew from the Clyde around the forecourt of Glasgow's new riverside Sheriff Court. The people who had already arrived at 1.30, thirty minutes before the time on their summons, were told to wait outside until 1.45, when the court would be open to the general public...

Six silent rows of involuntary witnesses listen intently as each defender is questioned. A visibly distressed woman who had to give up her job to nurse her husband is assured by the Sheriff that provided she starts paying instalments she won't lose her house. A woman alcoholic, the subject of neighbour's complaints, is eloquently pled for by a niece who explains she is now on a treatment programme.

A middle-aged man, his eyes red-rimmed, listens to the solicitor handling district council cases explain that his debt now runs to more than £900. The sheriff sternly warns that he must make some impact on this huge debt. Outside the court, still shaken, the man tells me that he also has fuel debts and can think of no way to meet the court's demands...

The sums involved that afternoon were often daunting: £500, £600, £700. The most common thread woven through stories of personal disaster, cash crises, redundancy and debt seemed to involve housing benefit. When the social security regulations changed in April many thousands lost part of their benefit – a combined rents and rates payment – and many lost any entitlement. The sudden need to make up that considerable shortfall seems to have blown sizeable holes in domestic budgets which already allowed no margins for unexpected expenditure.

(source: *The Scotsman*, 29 September 1988.)

Today's typical household

THE handbook also contains a mass of statistical information about life in Britain at the start of 1989.
- Two thirds of households own a car and a fifth have two or more.
- All but 2 per cent of households own a TV and 90 per cent have a colour set. Average viewing time is 28 hours per week.
- Nearly three quarters of households have central heating, 83 per cent own a washing machine and 83 per cent have a telephone.
- The average size of households is now just over 2.5 compared with 3 in 1961 and 4 in 1911. A quarter of households consist of one person.
- Cigarette smoking is the greatest preventable cause of death, accounting for 100,000 premature deaths annually but smoking is on the decline – 35 per cent of men and 31 per cent of women are smokers compared with 52 and 41 per cent respectively in 1972.
- 5,100 people were killed on roads in 1987, the lowest total since 1954.
- Savings are 5.4 per cent of income, compared with 13.8 per cent in 1980.
- Average weekly earnings in April 1987 were £224 for men and £148 for women.
- Two out of three people read a national morning newspaper and three out of four read a Sunday paper.

(source: *The Independent*, 3 January 1989.)

Q UESTIONS

1. What is the main factor in deciding what kind of lifestyle people have?
2. What differences can you find between the two couples in the chart:
   a) in income; b) in clothes?
3. What events could cause someone to get into debt?
4. What might the results be of getting into debt?
5. In what ways has the lifestyle of the average Briton changed in recent years?

A CTIVITIES

1. Form into groups of about four, to find more details about 'the budget'.
2. Study the chart, 'How the couples live'.
3. Can you construct a chart with headings similar to this one and fill it in for 'An unemployed couple'?
4. Study the 'Debt trap' item. Write a short dramatic scene for four characters, a judge, a prosecuting lawyer and a couple in debt, entitled, 'The Trial.'
5. What changes does your group think will have taken place in the average Briton's lifestyle in ten years time? Write down your ideas.
6. Nominate a spokesperson for each group.
7. The spokesperson should read out each groups' ideas for 'Future Britons.'
8. Discuss any similarities and/or differences in the ideas put forward by each group.

Contrasts in housing

EDINBURGH

erlooking the fairways of The Royal Burgess
Bruntsfield Golf Courses. Within easy driving
ance of the motorway network and the airport.
ar garage. Offers over £450,000. SWIMMING
OL COMPLEX.

s exceptional home offers generously
portioned accommodation with full central
ating and double glazing. Very high quality
ngs and fixtures. Full security system.
trance Vestibule, Cloakroom/Shower room,
ception Hall with marble floor, split level
awingroom incorporating entertaining area and
ors to Sun Terrace, Galleried Diningroom,
xury Kitchen with Dining/Breakfast room, Utility
oom, Master Bedroom Suite with Shower room
d Cloakroom. Two further Bedrooms with en
ite facilities, Sittingroom/Billard Room, Granny/
aff flat with Bedroom and Bathroom.

CRAIL

Outstanding positioned Flat in the attractive village
of Crail, nine miles from St Andrews. Sea views
from all windows of this exceptionally comfortable
3/4 roomed Flat. Large lounge/dining room with
picture windows affording views over garden and
sea. 2 double bedrooms with fitted wardrobes,
beautifully fitted kitchen, large utility room, modern
half tiled bathroom. Gas central heating
throughout, garage. All carpets and curtains.
Offers over: £47,000.
Rateable value: £768.
For details tel: (after 2 pm).

EDINBURGH

Modernised top floor Flat with vacant possesion.
Comprises hall, open plan livingroom/kitchen,
double bedroom and bathroom with coloured suite.
White meter electric heating. Mortgage available.
Viewing by arrangement with selling agents.
Further particulars from and offers over £17,000 to:

BANFFSHIRE
Portsoy

uated within a stone's throw of the quaint
rbour area in the lovely Village of Sandend, this
operty would make an ideal holiday or retirement
me. The accommodation is on two floors and
mprises on the ground floor: livingroom with
hen area off, bedroom and on the first floor: 2
c bedrooms and toilet.
ry realistically priced at offers over £12,000.
viewing arrangements and Schedule of
ticulars contact:

BATHGATE

Well maintained end terr Villa in a popular
residential area. The accommodation comprises
lounge/diningroom, fitted kitchen, bathroom, 2 dble
bedrooms (fitted wardrobes), gas c/h, gardens. O/o
£26,000.

ACTIVITIES

1. Study the advertisements, 'Houses for Sale.'

2. Write down a list of the houses, in order, from the most expensive to the least expensive.

3. Draw a line through your list, dividing off the houses which cost more than £200 000 from the others.

4. Draw a line through your list, dividing off the houses under £20 000 from the others.

5. Write down the main items which make a house worth a) over £200 000, and b) under £20 000.

6. Collect, from magazines and newspapers, some 'Houses for Sale' advertisements for your area.

7. Why might the same house be a different price a) in different parts of a town and b) in different parts of Scotland?

8. What are the advantages and disadvantages of renting a house or flat?

9. Can you find from newspapers and magazines some rent charges for flats per month?

10. Find advertisements which use the following words: a) A **detached** house; b) A **semi-detached** house; c) A **terraced** house; d) A **mortgage**; e) A **building society**. What do these words mean?

Contrasts in housing

'HOME, SWEET HOME'

In some cases, there are even greater contrasts in housing than those already mentioned. For some people, who can afford it, a very expensive house is part of their lifestyle.

THE HOMELESS

Some people cannot choose between buying an expensive house or buying a small flat. They cannot choose between types of rented accommodation, either. These people, for a variety of reasons, have no home of their own. They are homeless.

The homeless

IN THE OPEN-TO-THE-WIND concrete crypt of London's South Bank the cold is bitter, horrible; it burns like acid on the skin. As Estragon and Vladimir perplex at the Lyttleton Theatre, flautists pipe at the Royal Festival Hall and film buffs stream from the back exit of the National Film Theatre, a crowd of 20 to 30 men stamp their feet, blow into their hands and wander to and fro. The film-goers gawk at the wanderers, who take care not to notice, and keep apart from each other, so as not to register that they have something in common – they're all waiting for soup.

Pitifully vivid in the stark glare of an overhead security light is a green blanket which has taken human form and is shuddering uncontrollably; by the blanket's fringe lies a jaunty blue blazer with gold buttons, perfect dress for the Rotary Club but piercingly pathetic here, on the hard concrete ground patchworked with puddles...

But the shuddering thing in the blanket is not purposeless; it too is waiting for soup.

Away from the glare a terraced street of cardboard-fronted hutches distinguishes itself in the gloom: Welcome to Cardboard City. Not dogs, not pigs, but people live here. Some of the hutch-dwellers are trying to sleep, but it can't be easy, with the cold and the clanking of the trains, the screech of car alarms and the wood-on-concrete clatter of the fanatic skateboarders, weaving and dodging only feet away. The racket is worsened by three bawling kids, in the tow of a woman who says she is looking for her husband: "He's got my child benefit card. He sometimes comes here for the soup."

(source: *New Statesman*, 18/25 December, 1 January 1988.)

QUESTIONS

1. For what reasons might people become homeless?
2. Not all homeless people 'live rough' as in the quotation. Where might homeless people find temporary accommodation?
3. What is 'Shelter'?

The North–South divide

In a number of ways there are variations in how people live in different parts of Britain. What tends to show up in a number of surveys, however, is a divide between the wealthier, south-eastern part of England and the rest of the UK.

Some parts of Britain are enjoying low unemployment to such an extent that towns in south-eastern England had, in 1989, full employment.

In other parts of Britain, however, such as the north of England, Scotland and parts of Wales, the standard of living and employment levels are not so high, despite some recent high-technology industrial expansion. Scotland and Wales still suffer from the effects of the closure of large works and factories.

Scotland last in survey of UK economic trends

By SIMON BAIN

SCOTLAND'S economic health, relative to that of the rest of Britain, has worsened since 1981 as the North-South divide has intensified, according to a survey which spotlights winners and losers in 1980s Britain.

Scotland, in last place, is well behind in an index which measures economic change in Britain's ten regions during the decade...

"The over-riding impression of the changes taking place in local economies since 1981 is clearly of the division between North and South," the authors write, "Clearly the South is not uniformly prosperous nor the North uniformly poor, but in statistical terms North and South do constitute very different populations of labour market areas, and there is remarkably little overlap in scores between the two,"

In the general index of prosperity, Scotland's best-performing area is Hawick, in 89th place out of 280, helped by a high rate of female employment and thus economic activity, followed by Aberdeen (108th), Edinburgh (134th) and Inverness (138th). At the bottom are Coatbridge and Airdrie (258th), Banff and Buckie (264th), Arbroath (267th) and Stranraer (275th).

South of the Severn-Wash line lies a block of areas boasting "Britain's strongest combinations of low unemployment, high labour force activity, specialisation in advanced industries, high-salary employment and expensive housing". Milton Keynes is by far the fastest growing town and 17 areas around London are highly privileged places which have made great progress during the 1980s, including Huntingdon, Newbury, Thetford, Hertford and Ware...

(source: *The Scotsman*, 6 January 1988.)

Letter from America

QUESTIONS

1. Where does the survey draw the line between North and South in the UK?

2. What evidence did the researchers use as a basis for their statistics?

3. How many places were surveyed in the UK?

4. Name the four areas that came out at the top of the UK list.

5. What does the survey *not* claim to measure?

6. Why might some of these items be important to a local area?

ACTIVITIES

1. Using an atlas, find where each of the places mentioned in the extract on this page is situated. Mark them on a blank map (see page 114).

2. For Scotland, list the four top places and the four lowest places, indicating their UK position.

3. Write two paragraphs describing 'The South'.

4. Design a poster or pamphlet cover for your local area, showing the possible benefits for a business company wishing to set up there.

5. Write a brief summary, to accompany the poster or as part of the pamphlet, outlining the advantages of your area to potential business companies.

6. Using a library, find out and list ways in which a Government can encourage industries and companies to move away from the South-east of England to other areas of the UK.

7. What was 'no more' in the Proclaimers' song about Bathgate, Linwood, and Lochaber? Write a letter of explanation of this to a friend in America.

Differences within groups

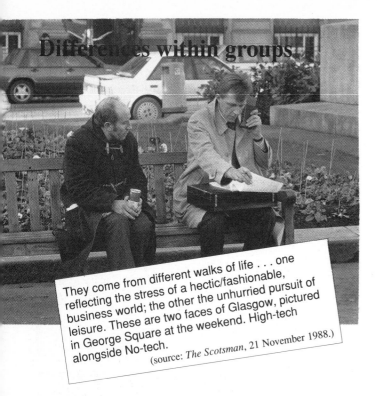

They come from different walks of life . . . one reflecting the stress of a hectic/fashionable, business world; the other the unhurried pursuit of leisure. These are two faces of Glasgow, pictured in George Square at the weekend. High-tech alongside No-tech.

(source: *The Scotsman*, 21 November 1988.)

As the previous survey suggested, not all parts of the 'Haves' regions are wealthy, and not all parts of the 'Have-Nots' regions are poor. Also there are groups who are near the average standard of living and some who are not. Even within the groups there may be wide differences. For example, compare the life of the pensioner below with that of the 'Glams' and 'Woopies' mentioned on pages 86 and 87.

Trying to keep warm, I have a wee cry . . .

BY MANDY RHODES

...With a total weekly income of £44.05, made up of the basic pension of £41.15 plus a top-up income support payment, Helen has every penny accounted for:

- £16.63 – contribution to rent, rates and some heating;
- £10 – to the SSEB towards her electricity bill;
- £1 – television licence stamp;
- £1.35 – to the lunch club;
- £1 – for bingo.

Total – £29.98, leaving Helen with just £14.07 to buy food, clothes, toiletries and any other necessities.

Helen suffered her second stroke a year ago and has been left partially paralysed and virtually deaf. She finds it difficult to wash and dress herself and needs to keep warm because she is no longer active. She receives no additional money to alleviate her health problems.

Her days are, she agrees, depressingly bleak. Waking at 7am she quickly pulls on the clothes that she has kept at the side of her bed. She rises, and after a roll and a steaming cup of tea she's ready to go out and sit in the local community centre for the day.

Returning at about 4pm, the elderly divorcee has a sandwich for tea and settles down in front of the television with a hot water bottle on her lap and duvet wrapped round her.

At 7pm it's too cold to sit any longer and Helen prepares for bed. Pulling on extra socks and a cardigan, she shivers as she pulls back the bedclothes.

Her days are boringly repetitive, spent mainly at the community centre. She says that without it she would quickly question the worth in her carrying on.

She said: "I go to the community centre as many days as I can and, although I have a free bus pass, I find the trek to a bus stop too much effort. And what would I do once I got out of the estate? I don't have the money to buy a cup of coffee in a cafe and what's the use of looking at things in shops I can't afford?

"The heating and lighting don't cost me anything at the centre. I attend the lunch club three days a week and meet friends for bingo on a Wednesday – the centre is a godsend and without it I would have nothing."...

(source: *Scotland on Sunday*, 27 November 1988.)

VARIATIONS IN ETHNIC GROUPS

There are variations in lifestyle and wealth not just between **ethnic groups** in the UK but also within different ethnic groups.

Out of work

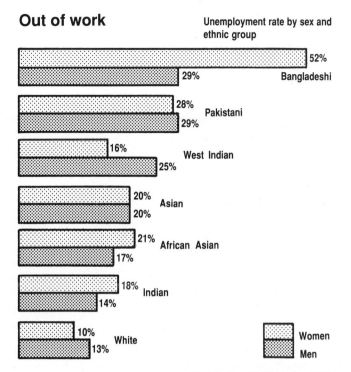

Unemployment rate by sex and ethnic group

- 52% / 29% — Bangladeshi
- 28% / 29% — Pakistani
- 16% / 25% — West Indian
- 20% / 20% — Asian
- 21% / 17% — African Asian
- 18% / 14% — Indian
- 10% / 13% — White

Women
Men

(source: *New Society*, 20 November 1987.)

QUESTIONS

1. Write a paragraph comparing the unemployment rate between:
   a) Pakistanis; b) West Indians.
2. What variations are there within each of these groups in terms of employment?
3. What differences are there between the two groups in terms of:
   a) professional jobs; b) housing?

Differing attitudes

Black and White, shown every night this week on BBC1, is a snapshot of everyday life. For the first time, the BBC used secret cameras to record the real attitudes of ordinary people in a typical British city. The reporters spent two months living incognito in Bristol, monitoring possible discrimination in jobs, accommodation, in pubs and clubs. 'We wanted to show what actually goes on,' says the series producer David Henshaw. 'What struck me most is the sheer banality of racial discrimination. Most of us, given the opportunity, have the capacity to be racists.'

Britain is not a 'wholly and deeply' racist society. What we do have is a large swathe of people who act in a small-minded and pernicious manner to anyone they deem 'different'.

(source: *The Listener*, 14 April 1988.)

ACTIVITIES

1. Form groups of four, to discuss the quotation 'Differing attitudes'. Do you agree with the last paragraph?
2. List some viewpoints agreeing or disagreeing with the statements.
3. Discuss your group's views with the other groups' views.

VIETNAMESE IN BRITAIN

...Housing and employment are the two major problems facing the Vietnamese in Britain today. Jobs are hard to come by. More than 80 per cent of Vietnamese of working age in Britain are unemployed. Those lucky enough to have found work are mostly employed in clerical work or catering. In Southwark a few small businesses, including a bakery, have been established. In Manchester, there is a jewellery shop and a few restaurants. But these are the exceptions.

Despite the immediate social problems of housing and work, the Vietnamese community is beginning to establish a sense of its own identity. Language classes, handicraft and art exhibitions, theatre and music recitals and a handful of vigorous magazines indicate strong attachment to culture and community. The latest 48-page issue of *Phu Nu Viet Nam*, a woman's magazine, contains poems, articles on women in Vietnamese history, pollution, Madonna, beauty care and news from Vietnam...

(source: *New Statesman & Society*, 20 November 1987.)

QUESTIONS

1. What percentage of Vietnamese people are unemployed in Britain?
2. What jobs have others found?
3. What housing problems face the Vietnamese people?
4. How do they keep a sense of community?

ACTIVITIES

Write two imaginary letters from Vietnamese schoolchildren living in Britain, one who is enjoying life here and one who is very unhappy.

KEYWORDS

The following Keywords are used in this Unit. Make sure you have understood what they mean.

lifestyles
standards of living
Haves, Have-Nots
poverty

budget
North-South divide
ethnic groups

7

CHANGE IN SOCIETY

TECHNOLOGY IN OUR LIVES

The meaning of technology

The photographs on this page show examples of the **new technology** which has become part of everyday life. '**Technology**' is all around us, but what do we mean by 'technology'?

Using the photographs to help you, write down one sentence to describe what *you* think is meant by 'technology'. Compare what you have written with others in your group or class and with a dictionary definition.

A useful short definition might be:

'Technology' refers to all the ways people use their inventions and discoveries to satisfy their needs. It involves the use of tools, machines, materials, techniques and different sources of power to make work easier and more productive.

Now look more closely at the photographs and answer the following questions for each photograph.

1. What benefits or advantages does the new technology have over the old method it has replaced?

2. Are there any disadvantages in using the new technology?

Technology and change

The introduction of new technology can bring about very big changes in people's lives. There are examples of the influence of new technology all around us – in the home, at school, in shops, in industry and offices, and in people's leisure and recreation activities. The activities on this page will help you to find out more about how technology affects you and your family.

A CTIVITIES

1. Carry out a survey in your own home, listing all the gadgets and machines which are examples of new technology. (Clue: the kitchen would be a good place to start.)

Opposite each item, write down the advantages and disadvantages of new technology. You may also wish to interview the people most affected by the changes.

2. In the school, interview the janitor, a selected number of teachers and other staff (perhaps in the school office), to find out how the introduction of modern technology has changed their work and affected their working conditions. (Remember there may be bad as well as good effects.) Your class teacher will be able to guide you in drawing up a suitable questionnaire, suggesting people to interview and how to conduct the interview.

3. If you live in a town or city, select a local factory or office and arrange a visit to interview the manager or a senior member of the staff about how changing technology affects their industry. (You might refer to sales, costs, number of employees, working conditions.)

If you live in a country area you could arrange to visit a local farm to interview the farmer or farm manager. After your visit you should write a short report and give a short talk to your class on your findings. You could send a copy of your report with a letter of thanks to the people you interviewed.

4. Look at the following examples of new technology. Draw up a chart like the one shown. Put a tick in the box opposite each one which you have in your home.

Now add up how many of the class have ticks opposite each example. Your teacher will help you to design a bar chart to show which examples are found more often than others. Discuss what you have found out about the influence of new technology in the homes of your class.

AUTOMATIC WASHING MACHINE	☐
ELECTRIC IRON	☐
VACUUM CLEANER	☐
ELECTRIC/GAS COOKER	☐
FRIDGE	☐
FREEZER	☐
ELECTRIC TOASTER	☐
ELECTRIC KETTLE	☐
COFFEE MAKER	☐
TUMBLE DRYER	☐
ELECTRIC DISHWASHER	☐
DIGITAL CLOCK or CLOCK/RADIO	☐
CASSETTE RECORDER	☐
TELEVISION	☐
MICROWAVE OVEN	☐
COMPACT DISC PLAYER	☐
TELEPHONE	☐
VIDEO RECORDER	☐
RECORD PLAYER	☐
PERSONAL STEREO (e.g. WALKMAN)	☐
CAMERA (STILL or VIDEO)	☐
TELETEXT	☐

KEYWORDS

The following Keywords are used in this Unit. Make sure you have understood what they mean.

new technology   'Technology'

THE IMPACT OF TECHNOLOGY

Sometimes the introduction of new technology can change the way industry works. On the next few pages you will see some examples of the impact of technology in industry and in the wider world.

Revolution in the supermarket

You will probably have noticed that many supermarkets now use electronic tills rather than the old manual tills which are still used in smaller shops. Here is an example of the latest till system being used by a supermarket chain company in its stores throughout the country. Look at the illustrations and read what the company says about its system.

SCANNING –
MAKING YOUR
SHOPPING EASIER

At our checkouts we are using the latest in computer technology to make your shopping easier – the SCANNING SYSTEM.

Scanning is a means of reading information contained by a product's bar code, which is the series of black lines and numbers found on most packs today. As each product is passed through the checkout the scanner reads the bar codes using a light beam. Precise, up to date information about each product which is held on a linked computer is recorded and printed on your receipt. The whole process takes a fraction of the time of the traditional, manual method and gives you a fully itemised receipt.

Our special cheque writer checkouts offer a further saving on your time too. The totalled amount will be printed for you along with the date and payee – all you need do is sign!

This fast and accurate system means that our products no longer have to be individually priced. You will, however, always find the price of each product clearly marked on the shelf edge. The shelf edge tickets also play an important part in product re-ordering and help us to keep our stores fully stocked.

An efficient system saves time for everybody. The saving to us is reflected in our prices so it's easy to see how you can save more than just time at Gateway.

gateway

· FULL · OF · FRESH · IDEAS ·

QUESTIONS

1. What is the system called?
2. Write down as many of the advantages this system has for shoppers as you can find.
3. What are the advantages for: a) the company, and b) the check-out operator, of the new system?

4. Are there any disadvantages for the customer or for the people employed by the company?
5. Why would you be unlikely to find this system in a small shop?

Changes in the newspaper industry

People in Britain read more newspapers than people in any other country in the world. In recent years there have been many changes in the method of newspaper production, and in how they look. More photographs, clearer print, smaller pages and in some cases the use of colour have made the finished product more attractive to readers. The owners of newspapers have also tried to produce more newspapers faster and more cheaply than ever before.

Newspapers such as *Today* use the most up-to-date technology in their production. This results in more eye-catching editions being produced more quickly and cheaply by fewer workers. Even some of the older newspapers such as *The Scotsman* now use modern techniques and machinery to speed up production, save money and produce a better quality of product.

The old and the new technology

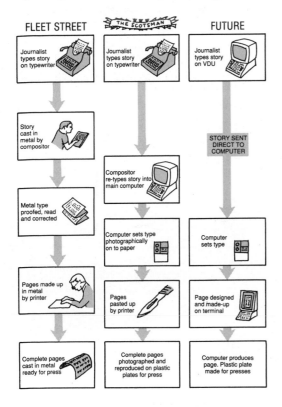

FLEET STREET | THE SCOTSMAN | FUTURE

- Journalist types story on typewriter
- Journalist types story on typewriter
- Journalist types story on VDU

- Story cast in metal by compositor
- STORY SENT DIRECT TO COMPUTER

- Metal type proofed, read and corrected
- Compositor re-types story into main computer

- Computer sets type photographically on to paper
- Computer sets type

- Pages made up in metal by printer
- Pages pasted up by printer
- Page designed and made-up on terminal

- Complete pages cast in metal ready for press
- Complete pages photographed and reproduced on plastic plates for press
- Computer produces page. Plastic plate made for presses

Industrial action, Wapping 1986

The diagram shows how the new methods are much simpler than the old ways, and involve fewer stages in the production of the newspaper.

Unfortunately, these changes have not always been acceptable to some groups of workers in the newspaper industry. Industrial action has been taken because the new methods require fewer workers and many people in the industry have lost their jobs.

Q UESTIONS

1. Why has new technology been introduced in the newspaper industry?

2. How does the new technology better satisfy the requirements of: a) the readers, and b) the owners, of newspapers?

3. Industrial action involving strikes and picketing offices was the result of some attempts to introduce new technology into the industry. Why did the workers react in this way?

The fishing industry

The industries which supply us with our food are very important, and any changes in these industries affect every one of us. In recent years the farming and fishing industries have begun to use more modern technology. The aim is to reduce the cost of producing food, increase the amount which can be produced, and improve the quality of food available for the consumer. The industries involved in food processing have also undergone many changes.

The fishing industry is a good example of how some of these changes work, but there may be other examples in your local area.

CASE STUDY: THE ORCADES VIKING II

The *Orcades Viking II* which is based in Stromness in the Orkney Islands is one of the biggest and most modern of the new 'high-tech' ships in the British fishing fleet.

'Orcades Viking II' has got the lot

by **Tim Oliver**

"THE SHIP which has everything" – that's the 190ft. super purser-trawler *Orcades Viking II* which began fishing last week after putting into Stromness – her home port in Orkney. Her crew can bask in every shipboard luxury including a sauna!

The seven-year-old former Norwegian vessel is in immaculate condition.She has been designed, built and finished to the highest possible standards in every department – deck, engineroom, wheelhouse and accommodation.

The 1,100-ton capacity, 2,500hp, super-ship is packed with just about every piece of technology available to a modern fishing vessel. As her skipper and major shareholder Angus Sinclair of Stromness said: "This is the ship of today."

The vessel must represent the biggest investment by individual fishermen, with no company involvement, in the UK fleet.

Skipper Sinclair declined to say how much the vessel had cost – "Let's just say she was expensive!" he said. But he estimated that to build her today would cost around £4.5m.

(source: Reproduced by kind permission of *Fishing News*, 19 September 1986.)

A traditional fishing boat and a 'high-tech' fishing ship at sea

Taking a 'catch'

ORCADES VIKING II left her home port of Stromness, Orkney, on the morning of Monday, September 1, and headed south-east through Scapa Flow in a strong westerly gale bound for the Pentland Firth and the southern North Sea.

The search for herring began in the area of Well Bank some 30 to 25 miles north-east of Cromer, on the Norfolk coast, on the Tuesday afternoon. Skipper Sinclair is using a Simrad ST sonar for long range searching and a Furuno CH12 colour sonar for close range tracking of shoals prior to shooting, both of which are "first class," he says.

He also uses a Furuno colour video sounder to help assess the size and density of the shoals – another excellent piece of equipment.

We soon pick up marks, but the skipper is undecided whether they are sufficiently dense to warrant shooting.

Skipper Sinclair decides it's worth a try and we shoot the 350-fathom x 85-fathom net in 30 fathoms, which means that "pursing" – drawing in the bottom of the net – begins as soon as possible to minimise bottom contact and any resulting damage to the net.

All methods of fishing have their moments of tension, anxiety and excitement – particularly when shooting and hauling – but none more so than purse seining. There is upwards of £100,000 worth of gear going over the side with every shot and, once shooting begins, there is no stopping. The whole pursing operation must be gone through, perhaps lasting an hour-and-a-half, even if there is no fish and no pumping.

...Eventually the purse is closed and the fish are alongside – and the skipper's anxieties once more turn to relief and satisfaction. We salvage a very respectable 280 tonnes from what he estimates was probably a haul of 700 or 800 tonnes and there is no damage to the gear.

The pumping operation is the most tedious aspect of pursing, especially with big hauls. Fish are pumped aboard at the rate of 100 to 200 tonnes an hour, depending on species and the type of pump, etc. While it can be a cold wet and boring job with big fishing in bad weather, it is nevertheless infinitely preferable to being "cold and bored gutting deckloads of little haddocks," as one crewman remarked.

(source: Reproduced by kind permission of *Fishing News*, 19 September 1986.)

The crew is highly appreciative of the vessel's comfort and spacious accommodation. "This ship is 'fishing de-luxe'," said one crew member, while another remarked that "It's hardly like being at sea."

The accommodation aboard *Orcades Viking II* can only be described as luxurious. A spacious messroom/recreation area is fitted with leather settees, engraved copper-faced tables, stainless steel fridge, coffee machine and TV.

The adjacent galley is fitted with 'all mod-cons,' including a potato peeler, dishwasher, foodmixer, microwave oven and stainless steel fridge. There is also a large walk-in fridge store, which contains two stainless steel deep-freeze units.

Accommodation is for 18 men in one and two-man berths. But with a crew of 12, each man will have a separate berth. The skipper, mate, engineer and cook's berths all have their own showers and toilets, the skipper and mate having leather settees. There is a large crew washroom area with showers and toilets and even a sauna is fitted. There is a sickbay, too.

(source: Reproduced by kind permission of *Fishing News*, 19 September 1986.)

A CTIVITIES

1.   Read the news items on the *Orcades Viking II*. Imagine you are writing a short article about the ship for a school magazine in which you are explaining the benefits of using the latest technology in the fishing industry. Your article should mention the benefits for the owners, the crew and the customers who buy fish in the shops. Can you also include some information about people who have suffered as a direct result of new technology in the fishing industry?

2.   Technology: good or bad? These three examples illustrate that the introduction of new technology does have an impact on people's lives. Sometimes that impact is good, but there are times when some individuals or groups suffer as a result. Collect press cuttings about people directly affected by new technology (e.g. people made redundant, 'yuppies') to make up your own mind on this question.

Q UESTIONS

What is meant by the phrase, 'high-tech' ship?

KEYWORDS

The following Keywords are used in this Unit. Make sure you have understood what they mean.

bar-code scanning   **'high-tech' ships**

Bringing Europe nearer

By the end of 1992, restrictions to free trade within the European Community will have been removed. Eurotunnel will open in 1993, at the right moment to provide a fixed link for the integrated Europe. Eurotunnel's shuttles and trains will serve the increasing freight and passenger markets, easing pressure on existing air and sea routes.

(source: Eurotunnel information leaflet)

Q UESTIONS

1. Describe how new technology will bring Britain closer to the rest of Europe in the 1990s.

2. Why is the building of the Eurotunnel important?

3. How will travellers benefit from the Eurotunnel in the 1990s?

4. Which groups of people might suffer as a result of the building of the new tunnel? (Some clues are given in the photograph.)

A CTIVITY

Find out more about the Eurotunnel project by writing to:
Eurotunnel Information Centre,
Tontine House,
Tontine Street,
Folkestone,
Kent CT20 1JR

THE IMPACT OF ECONOMIC CHANGE

Case Study

'SILICON GLEN'

* DISCO EQUIPMENT * 'JUMBO JETS' *
* PERSONAL COMPUTERS * MICROWAVE OVENS *
* SUBMARINES * RADAR SYSTEMS *

What do all of these things have in common?
The answer is that they all rely on the products of the electronic revolution which is all around us.

'Silicon Glen' is the name given to the area of Scotland in which many electronic companies have set up factories in recent years. These factories are mainly in the central area of Scotland, around Glasgow, Edinburgh and the New Towns (see map). A number of other areas such as the Borders can also claim to be part of 'Silicon Glen'.

The name comes from **silicon**, a material which is widely used in the electronics industry. The name is similar to 'Silicon Valley' in California which was the world's first and largest centre of the electronics revolution. The industry makes many products, including computers and parts (or **components**) for computers and other electronic machines.

Twenty years ago the industry was very small. Today, it employs more than 46 000 people in Scotland, many of them working in factories owned by Japanese

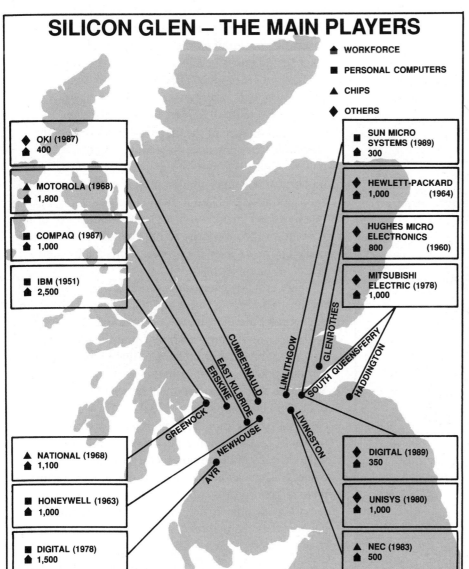

The breadth of the industry in Scotland is illustrated by the product list shown below.

Alarm systems
Computers
Control equipment
Disc drives
Electronic instruments
Heart pacemakers
Military equipment
Navigation aids
Opto-electronics
PCBs
Personal computers
Radar systems
Semiconductors
Sonar equipment
Telecommunications
Transformers
Underwater cameras
Workstations

(*Sunday Times*, Scotland, 2 July 1989, Page 2.)

or American companies (over 20 per cent of those employed). These foreign companies have been attracted to Scotland for three main reasons:

1. Scotland is ideally placed for the European market which will become increasingly important when trade barriers are removed in 1992.
2. Scottish workers have many of the skills needed in the electronics industry – skills involving putting very small components together with great accuracy. These skills have been developed through a long history of engineering, textiles and similar industries in Scotland and because of high unemployment there are many workers available.
3. The Government has given money, **incentives**, to foreign companies willing to set up factories in Scotland to provide jobs.

A LEADING EUROPEAN CENTRE

Scotland is a beautiful country renowned for its scenic graneur. The environment is clean and unpolluted and one is never far from the picturesque highlands or the rugged coastline. Scotland is ideally positioned for worldwide communications, with 5 international airports and major motoring networks and seaports.
Despite being in a relatively small country with a population of 5 million, the electronics community has a 42000 strong workforce in around 300 companies, many of whom are international names. In large multi nationals like IBM, DEC, Ferranti and Motorola and the many smaller support companies, more than 15000 new jobs have been created over the last five years. It all adds up to a massive £400 million worth of investment which has made Scotland a major centre in World Electronics.

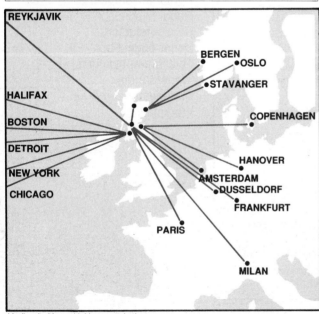

Ideally suited for worldwide communications

(source: 'Electronics, the state of the art in Scotland', Scottish Development Agency, 1988.)

In the south of "Silicon Glen" is the Scottish Borders. Over the past twenty-five years the Scottish Borders has developed into a major centre for high quality/high technology electronics. The region's electronic industry involves some twenty-five companies employing around 1600 people. Most of these companies are concentrated in three towns: Galashiels, Kelso and Selkirk. The region now contains the largest concentration of high quality/high technology printed circuit board (PCB) manufacturing in Europe. Whether it's in the front line of defence or the High Street bank the chances are that advanced electronic equipment contains PCBs made in the Scottish Borders.

Without the investment made by the electronics industry, Scotland would be very much poorer. Many of our major industries, e.g. coalmining, shipbuilding and heavy engineering, which used to employ many thousands of people, are now much smaller. In some cases, like coalmining, the industry has almost disappeared either because there has been a fall in the demand for its products, because it cannot produce cheaply enough, or because it cannot compete with the prices and quality of similar foreign products.

The importance of the electronics industry to the economic develoment of Scotland cannot be underestimated. Wages in the industry are usually higher than average, and the money earned is spent in shops, on new cars and in buying houses, bringing much needed income to many communities. All of this is good for the prosperity of the country and helps to make up for some of the problems created by high levels of unemployment.

There are, however, some problems connected with the strong foreign influence in the industry. Electronics is a world-wide industry. Goods made in Scotland are sold throughout Europe, in the United States of America, and even in Japan. But these countries also sell their electronic goods in the world marketplace. When the demand for products falls and large multinational companies are looking for ways of cutting costs and saving money, very often they close down **'branch' factories** abroad in order to protect their own workers' jobs in their main factories in their own country. This can happen even if the 'branch' factory is making good profits. Many of Scotland's electronic factories are 'branch' factories and are therefore in danger when the market is not strong. A recent example of the closure of such a factory was the Wang factory in Stirling.

Wang pulls plug on Stirling

Outcry as US company axes 240 computer jobs

The WANG computer factory at Stirling, hailed on its opening in 1984 as a triumph of inward investment and a symbol of hope for the Scottish electronics industry, is to close with the loss of all 240 jobs.

Wang's decision, broken to the non-union workforce yesterday, provoked a cross-party outcry and brought calls from many quarters for the Government to attach more stringent conditions to inward investment incentives to avoid the establishment of vulnerable branch plants with minimal Scots roots.

The company is thought to have received close to £5 million in construction aid for a £38 million enterprise initially projected to employ 700 people assembling desk-top personal computers. A £3.5 million extension to the plant was opened recently.

Last night, the company confirmed from its head office in Massachusetts that the Stirling operation would close, and that its output would be transferred to Wang's Irish plant at Limerick, which currently concentrates on office information systems. The closure decision had been taken with "great reluctance".

(source: *The Scotsman*, 27 June 1989.)

Q UESTIONS

1. What is 'Silicon Glen'?
2. Why have many electronics companies set up in Scotland?
3. What benefits has the industry brought to Scotland?
4. Are there any problems in the development of the industry in Scotland?

A CTIVITY

Using the map on page 125, choose one of the electronics companies close to your school. Build up a 'Fact-File' on the company, using as many different ways of collecting information as possible (letters, interviews, reading publicity pamphlets etc.).

Your file should contain information about when and why the company set up in Scotland; what it makes and where it sells its products; how many people it employs and how much its annual wage bill is; how it is involved in the local community and what its plans are for the future.

Your file may take the form of a folder of information or a wall display by your group or class.

KEYWORDS

The following Keywords are used in this Unit. Make sure you have understood what they mean.

silicon   incentives
components   'branch' factories

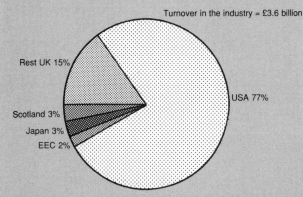

MARKETS
(MANUFACTURING COMPANIES)

SHARE OF ELECTRONICS TURNOVER
BY HEAD OFFICE LOCATION

Turnover in the industry = £3.6 billion

Rest UK 15%
USA 77%
Scotland 3%
Japan 3%
EEC 2%

This shows the turnover of the industry by head office location. US companies contribute 77% of turnover, Scottish owned companies 3%.

The EEC is the single most important market place for electronic goods produced in Scotland and accounts for almost 80% of total output. The home marketplace, Scotland and the rest of the UK, accounts for 7% and 26.5% respectively.

Scottish Development Agency
ELECTRONICS DIVISION
NOV 1988

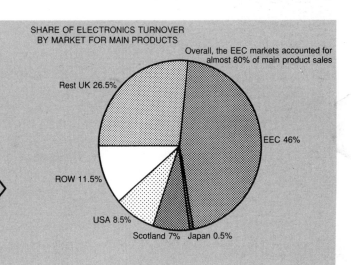

SHARE OF ELECTRONICS TURNOVER
BY MARKET FOR MAIN PRODUCTS

Overall, the EEC markets accounted for almost 80% of main product sales

Rest UK 26.5%
EEC 46%
ROW 11.5%
USA 8.5%
Scotland 7%
Japan 0.5%

INDEX